ECHOES FROM A GOD

ECHOES FROM A GOD

Diego Maradona

The Manager and his Post-Playing Life

ROB SMITH

pitch

First published by Pitch Publishing, 2026
1

Pitch Publishing
9 Donnington Park, 85 Birdham Road
Chichester, West Sussex, PO20 7AJ
www.pitchpublishing.co.uk
info@pitchpublishing.co.uk

Set in Adobe Caslon 11/15pt

Typeset by Pitch Publishing

Cover design by Olner Design

The authorised representative in the EEA is
Easy Access System Europe OÜ, Mustamäe tee 50, 10621 Tallinn, Estonia gpsr.requests@easproject.com

A CIP catalogue record for this book is available from the British Library

ISBN 978 1 83680 437 6

Contents

Introduction

THERE ARE men who live two lives. Diego Armando Maradona lived three, perhaps four. He lived as a boy from Villa Fiorito, chasing a ball on dirt pitches, dreaming of lifting his family from poverty. He lived as a footballer – the greatest of his generation. Some argue, the greatest to ever play the sport.

He dazzled crowds as a teen for Argentinos Juniors, brought joy and far more attention to himself when he played for his beloved Boca Juniors, before becoming a world-record signing when he moved to Barcelona in 1982. His time in Catalonia wasn't his favourite. Immediately a marked man, injury and illness limited his brilliance. His final game for the club ended in a mass brawl with kicks and punches thrown in the Copa del Rey final between Barça and Athletic Bilbao, with Diego at the centre of it. His gifted style of play ensured another world-record fee to Napoli, where he dazzled crowds and became a god in the Italian city, leading the team to some silverware. He won the World Cup in 1986 and was regarded by fans, journalists, pundits and his peers as the world's greatest player.

After leaving Napoli in 1991, Diego Maradona's career entered a turbulent final chapter marked by flashes of brilliance overshadowed by controversy. A 15-month suspension for failing a drug test cut short his time in Italy, and his return to Spain with Sevilla in 1992 was brief, featuring only a handful of standout performances before tensions with management hastened his exit. He returned to his home country and joined Newell's Old Boys in 1993, but injuries and fitness struggles limited his impact. Maradona still made his way to the 1994 World Cup with Argentina, where he produced a moment of vintage magic against Greece before testing positive for ephedrine and being sent home in disgrace. In 1995, he played his final club football with Boca Juniors, officially retiring two years later.

He lived as an addict, enslaved by cocaine, seduced and betrayed by fame, lurching from crisis to crisis in nights of excess that nearly killed him. And finally, when his playing career ended, he lived as a coach, a manager, a figure on the sideline who carried all those lives within him – the genius, the addict, the survivor – pacing touchlines across Argentina, South Africa, Dubai, Mexico and La Plata. His coaching years were not a clean epilogue, but a messy continuation, a final act in a drama that never truly found peace.

To speak of Maradona as a manager without speaking of his demons is to miss the truth. His appointments were always shaped by the question of survival: could he keep his health intact; could he escape his addictions long enough to work; could his heart hold out? He nearly died in January 2000 in Punta del Este, Uruguay, collapsing from a cocaine-induced heart attack that left him in intensive care for days. He nearly died again in 2004, when his body, swollen and exhausted from years of abuse, gave way and forced him back into hospital. Those images – of him unconscious, intubated, his family weeping outside clinics – became part of his mythology as surely as the Hand of God or the goals against England. Diego the indestructible, Diego the survivor, Diego who cheated death again and again. Each time he returned, frailer perhaps, but still burning with defiance. Each time, Argentina sighed with relief, as though a god had been restored to earth.

These health battles left scars that followed him into his managerial career. He was never a picture of calm fitness on the sidelines. He was often overweight, his face puffy, his body bearing the strain of decades of addiction and abuse. Yet he carried himself with the same volcanic charisma, the same restless energy. He could no longer run like the boy of Villa Fiorito, but on the touchline he moved with a kind of nervous urgency, as though trying to keep death itself at bay through sheer motion. Coaching, for him, was not only about football. It was about staying alive, about staying inside the game that gave him meaning. Without football, he drifted into nights that nearly killed him. With football, he had purpose, family, theatre. His managerial career cannot be separated from this existential struggle.

It is tempting to see his coaching record purely through the lens of results, and on that basis, it is cruel. At Deportivo Mandiyú, he only won a single match. At Racing Club, he lasted only 11 games. With

Argentina at the 2010 World Cup, he oversaw one of the country's most painful defeats, a 4–0 demolition by Germany. In Dubai with Al Wasl, in Fujairah, in Mexico with Dorados, in La Plata with Gimnasia, the pattern was the same: brief moments of joy, long stretches of inconsistency, no trophies. He was mocked as a tactician, dismissed as a showman, ridiculed for relying on hugs and slogans instead of systems and strategies. And yet, this cold arithmetic misses what was truly happening.

For Maradona, coaching was never about diagrams on a board. It was about theatre, about passion, about love. He coached as he lived: with his heart in his throat, with his arms wide open, with tears in his eyes. He hugged his players as though they were his children. He kissed Messi on the forehead before matches in South Africa, whispered encouragement into his ears. He told journeymen in Corrientes to believe they could conquer giants. He gave freedom to talents at Racing who had been shackled by fear. He defended his squads against the press, shielded them from criticism and carried their failures as his own. To play under Diego was not to receive tactical blueprints, but to feel embraced by history itself.

The paradox was brutal. His charisma could inspire, but it could not organise. His love could comfort, but it could not protect against opponents who were fitter, faster, more disciplined. And so his teams struggled. They reflected his life: flashes of brilliance, collapses of chaos, yet an unforgettable spectacle.

Behind the sidelines, the old battles raged. Diego's health haunted every chapter. He coached Dorados in Mexico while hobbling on damaged knees, sometimes forced to sit in a golf cart to issue instructions. At Gimnasia, in his final job, he appeared frail, leaning on assistants, his body visibly failing. He had survived the tricky combination of global fame and addiction, but his body carried the cost – heart disease, high blood pressure, the toll of excess. Every time he collapsed into hospital, Argentina held its breath. Every time he returned to the bench, they celebrated as though he had scored another goal. His life was measured not only in matches but in recoveries, in escapes from death, in battles won against his own body.

He was vocal about certain issues as well. And people listened. With his leftist views, he spoke out in support of Palestine and sported tattoos of Che Guevara and Fidel Castro. Each time he spoke, it was box office. The press took note of everything. His fame gave him the platform to champion the underdog, for people who came from the similar humble, working-class background from which he was raised.

On the sidelines, despite the defeats, despite the ridicule, despite the frailty, his managerial career mattered. It mattered because it kept him alive, kept him in the embrace of football, kept him connected to the people who adored him. It mattered because it revealed him fully, stripped of the ball, exposed as man and myth. It mattered because it gave Argentina a chance to love him again, not only for goals but more so for his presence. Every stadium he entered, every touchline he paced, every press conference he stormed, was another act in a play that had no ending. To so many, Diego was a god.

This book is an attempt to tell that story – not of triumphs, but of survival; not of tactics, but of humanity and the adoration he enjoyed since he was a teenager. From Mandiyú in Corrientes to Racing in Avellaneda, from the World Cup in South Africa to the deserts of Dubai, from narco-land Sinaloa to his final chapter in La Plata, this is the story of Maradona as a manager. It is not a story of trophies because sadly there were none. It is a story of myth, of theatre, of a man who refused to disappear, who fought to the last breath to remain inside the game he loved, who turned even failure into legend.

And it is also the story of his shadows: drug- and alcohol-fuelled nights, the collapses in hospital, the tears of his daughters, the fear of a nation every time the word 'Maradona' and 'emergency' appeared in the same headline. His post-playing life and career cannot be told without these shadows, because they followed him on to every sideline, into every press conference, into every embrace. They were part of him, as much as his genius and his charisma. To tell the story of Maradona the manager is to tell the story of a man who lived at the edge of death and refused to fall.

CHAPTER ONE

An Experiment for a God

A DARK car tore along National Route 12, the horizon bleeding under a rust-coloured sky. Corrientes dozed in the heat – shuttered shops on Avenida Pedro Ferré, paint bleached and curling in the sun. Then, as the car swung on to Avenida Sarmiento, the silence fractured. Horns blared. Drums rattled. Someone started chanting his name. The noise rolled through the streets like a sudden squall. Diego Armando Maradona had arrived.

He stepped out wearing dark glasses, a silver chain catching the light, and, for a moment, time snapped back to the days when every lens in the world pointed at him. The flashes went off like fireworks. He looked leaner, older, but ready for work. The crowd surged, half-mad with joy – *¡Dios!* they shouted, *¡Gracias por venir!* It wasn't often that the footballing gods took a detour to Corrientes. His grin – the same one that once lit up Napoli's San Paolo and Boca's La Bombonera – flickered to life again. He waved, once, twice, as if embarrassed by the adoration but also fuelled by it.

Corrientes wasn't Naples and it wasn't Buenos Aires. The city sat quietly on the eastern shore of the Paraná River, not far from the Paraguayan border, but relatively far from the epicentre of global sport. Some of his family were already familiar with the city; it's where his parents lived before moving to Villa Fiorito before he was born.

The Estadio José Antonio Romero Feris was a modest ground hemmed in by mango trees and low houses, its stands patched and uneven. But on this day, it was the centre of the footballing world. Inside, the pitch was rough, scorched by the northern sun – part grass, part dust, but no one cared. A boy in sandals tugged at his father's sleeve, whispering that Maradona was really here. The father didn't reply. He just crossed himself and stared, as if the sight alone required faith.

For Diego, this was something of a gamble. It was meant to be a beginning – a first step back into the game that had both made and destroyed him. The ban, the suspensions, the exile – all of it hung around him like invisible smoke. Yet as he walked on to that imperfect provincial pitch, clutching a clipboard instead of a ball, he looked lighter than he had in years. The crowd sang his name. Somewhere in that song, he heard forgiveness. 'Football,' as he often said, 'is what saves me.'

The club was Deportivo Mandiyú, a modest side struggling in Argentina's Primera División, desperate for salvation, desperate for attention, desperate for something – or someone – to change their fate. The name itself carried a certain poetic quality. Mandiyú, meaning 'cotton' in the indigenous Guaraní language, spoke of roots, of earth, of something fragile and humble. For a team staring at relegation, survival seemed unlikely.

What they needed, their directors thought, was not just a coach but a miracle. In the summer of 1994, the club had been in financial dire straits, which resulted in its sale for $2 million. With the new owners looking to make an immediate impact, they couldn't have chosen a more high-profile manager.

Maradona, in the aftermath of his expulsion from the 1994 World Cup in the United States for a doping violation for which he was banned from football for 15 months, seemed to need something too. Management offered him a way back into football without stepping on to the pitch, a way to channel his presence, his passion, his obsession. And for Mandiyú, bringing him in was as much about spectacle as about results. Imagine the headlines: Diego Maradona, world champion, taking charge of a small provincial club. It was absurd. It was surreal. And for that very reason, it seemed perfect.

The deal was announced in October 1994. The press exploded. In Buenos Aires, editors scrambled to redesign front pages. Radio shows buzzed with incredulity. Television stations dispatched crews to make the 1,000km drive from the capital to Corrientes to cover every detail. The absurdity of it all only added to the fascination. Diego Maradona, the man who had once conquered the world in Mexico, who had lifted the World Cup, who had enthralled Naples, was now the manager of Mandiyú, a team whose stadium held barely 15,000 people, whose budget was minuscule, whose players were journeymen and hopefuls. It was like a fallen emperor returning not to a palace but to a farmhouse, not to a throne but to a wooden bench. And yet, for Argentina, the story was irresistible.

When Diego arrived in Corrientes, the city erupted. Crowds lined the streets, waving flags, shouting his name, climbing on to rooftops for a glimpse. It was not just a new coach arriving; it was Diego Maradona, myth and man, sinner and saint, walking through their streets. He was joined at the club by former River Plate goalkeeper Sergio Goycochea, who had worn Argentina's number one shirt at the recent World Cup. Such an addition to the squad cemented the new owners' desire for results.

Club officials weren't entirely sure of what vision Maradona would bring to the club. Some columnists praised him for returning to the game in any capacity; others warned that Mandiyú were chasing spectacle rather than salvation.

For the people of Corrientes – distant from the glitter and noise of Buenos Aires – his arrival felt like a visitation, a small-town miracle wrapped in dust and heat. It was part carnival, part resurrection. They didn't see a fallen idol or a man exiled from football's grand stages; they saw their own son coming home, flawed but luminous. When he stepped from the car, time seemed to ripple, the air charged with something both sacred and impossible to name. He gave them dignity simply by choosing them, by standing there in their midst. In return, they gave him what he had always needed most: unconditional love.

From the very first training session, the mayhem was obvious. Cameras surrounded the pitch. Reporters filled the stands. Players such as the Bolivian defender Luis Cristaldo, Paraguayan midfielder Guido 'El Mago' Alvarenga, and striker Carlos Casartelli were unused to this level of press attention, and found themselves photographed, interviewed and analysed.

Diego, in an Adidas t-shirt, whistle around his neck, tried to play the role of coach. He gestured, shouted, embraced, encouraged. But it was clear from the beginning that he was not a tactician. His instructions were vague, emotional, instinctive. He told defenders to fight, attackers to dribble, midfielders to run. He spoke in slogans, in metaphors, in passion. For the players, it was surreal. They had idolised him as children, watched him conquer the world, and now he was their coach. To be scolded by Diego, to be hugged by Diego, to be told to run harder by Diego, was both intimidating and exhilarating.

His debut as a manager came on 9 October 1994, against Rosario Central. The stadium, the Estadio José Antonio Romero Feris was in its infancy, having been inaugurated just eight years prior, and it was packed. Every seat taken, every vantage point occupied. People climbed trees outside to glimpse the pitch. Maradona had to watch the game from the stands. He was not calm, not composed. He lived every moment as though he were still a player, as though he could run on to the field himself. He watched in a shirt and tie with a white plastic chair beneath him, animated and vocal.

Photographers pointed their lenses at him throughout, instead of at the pitch.

Diego wasn't on the sidelines as he lacked the formal managerial licence to be beside Carlos Fren, directing the players from the dugout.

The match itself ended in a 1–2 loss. There was nothing extraordinary in the football, but the atmosphere was electric. Every gesture of Diego was magnified. When he shouted encouragement, the crowd roared. At full time, he took to the pitch to shake the hands of all the players. Despite the loss, the true result for the club's fans was the sight of Diego Maradona, world champion, as their manager.

The weeks that followed, however, exposed the reality. Mandiyú unfortunately were a weak team, their squad limited, their confidence fragile. Diego, for all his passion, could not invent quality where it did not exist. His instructions were emotional but rarely strategic. He urged players to give everything, but 'everything' was not enough in Argentina's Primera División. The defeats came quickly, each one sharper than the last. The press, once intoxicated by the novelty, began to turn. They analysed his mistakes, mocked his tactical confusion and ridiculed his record. The club's new owners were on his back also. Diego, as always, responded with defiance. He said the team lacked luck, that the referees were against them, that the players fought bravely. He took the criticism personally, as though it were not about Mandiyú but about him, about his honour, about his name.

Still, in those months of 1994, something important happened. Diego Maradona, disgraced and suspended, found a way back into football. He was not a good coach, not even an average one. But he was there, on the sideline, living the game, feeling its pulse, breathing its air. For a man who could not exist outside of football, that was survival. For Mandiyú, though relegation loomed, his presence gave them a place in history. They became the team that Maradona once managed, the team that carried his myth for a brief, wild autumn.

The Mandiyú players adored him personally but struggled to adapt to his methods. Training sessions were often improvised, more motivational speech than tactical plan. Diego would gather them in a huddle, his voice booming, his arms gesturing, his eyes alive. He told them to fight, to love the shirt, to play with heart. He told them stories of Mexico 1986, of how belief had carried Argentina to glory. He promised them that if they gave everything, miracles could happen. For a moment, in the warmth of his words, they believed. But when the whistle blew, belief without structure faltered. Opponents passed around them, organised and precise. Mandiyú, for all their heart, were exposed.

It became apparent early on that Maradona's appointment was less about building a competitive team and more about generating attention. His presence was a commercial strategy – a way to fill the stands, sell shirts and put a struggling club back on the map. Carlos Fren, his assistant, later reflected that Maradona operated almost entirely on instinct and emotion, rarely on structured planning. The coaching staff, he said, did their best to channel that intensity into something more coherent on the training ground. Yet the truth was obvious to anyone watching: Maradona's real value lay not in tactics, but in magnetism.

The defeats came quickly and painfully. Against Vélez Sarsfield, against Independiente, against River Plate, Mandiyú were outclassed. The players fought, ran, sweated, but quality told. Maradona stood on the touchline, gesticulating wildly, shouting encouragement, berating referees, waving at the crowd. The cameras loved him, the fans adored his passion, but the scoreboard was merciless. Mandiyú slid towards the bottom of the table, their survival slipping away.

The press, which had once celebrated the absurdity of his appointment, now circled like vultures. They mocked his record, analysed his decisions, replayed his post-match interviews with irony. They accused him of being more showman than coach, more circus than strategy. They said Mandiyú had hired not a manager but a spectacle, and now they were paying the price. Diego, stung, lashed out. In press conferences he insulted journalists, accused them of bad faith and reminded them of his glories. He said they would never forgive him for being Maradona, that they hated him because he was who he was. The battle between Diego and the press became as much a part of the story as the matches themselves.

Yet even in the defeats, the crowds did not abandon him. In Corrientes, the people continued to fill the stands and chant his name. For them, results were secondary. To have Diego Maradona in their city, wearing their badge, pacing their sideline, was worth more than victories. They treated him not as a failed coach but as a miracle in flesh, proof that their small club mattered. When he shouted at the referees, they roared with him. When he embraced players after losses, they cheered his compassion. He gave them dignity by choosing them and they gave him devotion in return.

Inside the dressing room, the atmosphere was complicated. Players were awed by his presence, grateful for his trust, but confused by his methods. Some longed for clear tactical guidance, for drills that would prepare them, for systems that would protect them. Instead, they received passion, fire and anecdotes. Some responded with loyalty, giving everything on the pitch. Others grew frustrated, feeling lost. But none could bring themselves to disrespect him. He was Diego. Even when his instructions were unclear, even when his choices baffled them, they obeyed, because disobedience to Maradona felt like sacrilege.

As the weeks went on, the spectacle around Mandiyú grew larger than the football itself. Every defeat, every outburst, every fragment of press conference drama was reported in exhaustive detail. National outlets that rarely looked north of Buenos Aires now treated the small Corrientes club as headline material, drawn less by performance than by the enduring magnetism of Diego Maradona. The attention was relentless. Corrientes was more used to quiet rhythms, and found itself under siege from cameras and correspondents. Hotels were booked solid, bars filled with talk-show punditry and every training session became a media event. For locals, it was intoxicating – their town at the centre of Argentina's football conversation. But behind the frenzy, the football was faltering. Mandiyú's results didn't match the noise and the gap between myth and reality grew wider by the week.

The press laughed cruelly, the pundits dismissed him as a disaster, rivals mocked. But Diego refused to resign. He insisted he would fight until the end, that he would not abandon his players, that he would prove everyone wrong. His defiance was heroic, but it was also tragic. He had walked into an impossible situation, and even his brilliance, even his myth, could not save it.

And yet, for all the defeats, for all the ridicule, something unforgettable had been created. Mandiyú, once a provincial club known only locally, was now etched into the history of Argentine football. They would always be remembered as the team Maradona managed, the team that carried his myth, however briefly. For Corrientes, those months were a carnival, a visitation, a moment of belonging to the larger story of Argentina. And for Diego, though the experience was painful, it gave him something vital: a way back into football, a reminder that the game still needed him, that even from the sideline, he could not be ignored.

For the players, the weight was suffocating. They were men of limited means and limited talent, many journeymen clinging to their place in the top division.

To carry Diego Maradona's name on their shoulders was both a blessing and a curse. It brought them fame, attention and moments of pride, but it also brought unbearable scrutiny. Each mistake they made was amplified, each missed pass or conceded goal replayed on national television not as their failure but as Maradona's. And in that strange inversion, they felt both invisible and overexposed. Some players, younger and wide-eyed, adored Diego's presence no matter what. To be in his orbit was enough. Others, older and hardened, grew quietly resentful. They needed structure, clarity, a coach who could prepare them for battle. Diego gave them passion, fire, belief – but no compass.

The defeats deepened. Mandiyú's matches became grim affairs, battles of desperation rather than contests of quality. They drew occasionally, clung to hope with last-minute goals, but the tide was against them. Their squad was simply not strong enough for survival. And Diego, who had once carried weak teams on his back as a player, could not perform the same miracle from the sideline. He raged on the touchline, shouted at referees, gestured wildly at his players, but the gulf in class remained.

The directors of Mandiyú, who had brought him in as a desperate gamble, now faced a dilemma. On the one hand, his presence had put their club on the map. They had sold tickets, filled stadiums and made headlines. On the other hand, the defeats were piling up, relegation loomed and their gamble looked reckless. Privately, some began to regret the appointment, admitting that the chaos had overwhelmed the football. But to dismiss him was unthinkable. Who would dare fire Maradona, the living legend, the world champion? Who would dare take on the anger of Corrientes, who adored him? The directors hesitated, caught between pragmatism and myth.

Diego himself began to show the strain. His face, always expressive, revealed fatigue. His voice, once booming with defiance, grew hoarser. The joy of his arrival had curdled into frustration. He loved his players, loved their fight, but he knew in his heart that they were outmatched. He could not dribble past rivals for them, could not conjure genius from nothing. He felt powerless, and Diego had never been powerless before. It gnawed at him, humiliated him, crushed him.

Yet he refused to resign. That was not his way. To resign would be to surrender, to admit defeat, to give his enemies the satisfaction. He told the press he would fight to the end, that he would not abandon Mandiyú, that he would go down with the ship if necessary. The words stirred some loyalty, but they could not change the results. Loss followed loss, the table grew darker, the hope dimmed.

His final matches as Mandiyú's coach were bleak. The stadium was still filled with fans, but the atmosphere was heavier, more mournful than festive. The people of Corrientes still sang his name, still adored him, but they too felt the inevitability of failure. Against Boca Juniors, his beloved Boca, Mandiyú were dismantled. Against Racing, they fought but lost. Against smaller clubs, they drew or faltered. Each week, the headlines sharpened, the critics louder.

Maradona sat alone in the tiny manager's office after yet another defeat, a room that smelled of grass, sweat and damp concrete. His shirt clung to his back. The walls were thin enough to hear the players showering, laughing uneasily, pretending not to care. On the desk, beside an untouched *mate*, lay a yellow notepad filled with scribbles – player numbers, half-formed tactics, names crossed out, rewritten, crossed out again. He stood, turned off the light and walked out into the heat. A handful of fans waited by the gate. One boy, no older than ten, ran up and handed him a ball to sign. Diego took it, scrawled his name and smiled with the weary tenderness of someone who knows the signature might mean more than the man.

After 12 games and only a single victory, the six draws and five defeats were the focus of the headlines. In December 1994, Maradona resigned as manager of Deportivo Mandiyú. The announcement came not with shock but with weary inevitability. The press reported it with a mix of scorn and fascination. Some called it a humiliation, others a farce, still others a lesson in the limits of myth. Diego, in his resignation statement, remained defiant. He said he had given everything, that his players had fought, that he was proud of them. He said he had been betrayed by luck, by referees, by fate. He insisted he had not failed, but that the circumstances had been impossible. A little over two months was hardly a great start to a managerial career, but at the same time, it wasn't really adequate time to prove his abilities.

For Corrientes, the months of Maradona's tenure became a chapter told with enduring pride. They remembered the days when the world's eyes briefly turned their way – when Diego Armando Maradona, suspended from playing and hungry to reinvent himself, walked their streets and stood in their dugout. For a provincial city used to the quiet, it felt like a visitation from mythology itself. The results were poor, but for some that was unimportant. What lingered was the memory of his presence: the flashes of charisma, the certainty that for a few fleeting weeks, their club had mattered on a national stage.

For the players, it was an education in both awe and chaos – to be coached by Maradona, even in failure, was to brush against history. He demanded intensity, emotion, belief, but his magic as a player could not be easily translated into management. For Diego, the experiment was deeply personal. He sought to recapture that old intoxication of control, of shaping the game, of feeling its pulse from close range. The dream outpaced the reality, yet the act itself – stepping back into football's arena, refusing to fade – was a kind of victory. In Corrientes, he failed as a coach but succeeded, once again, in being impossible to ignore.

In the end, the truth was self-evident: Maradona had never been a conventional coach. His methods at Mandiyú were instinctive, emotional, often improvised – less a tactical project and more a burst of Diego himself, imposed on a club that needed structure far more than spectacle. And when the spell ended, after just a handful of matches, he slipped back into a kind of limbo. For weeks he floated on the edges of the Argentine game – giving the odd interview, appearing at training grounds, dropping hints to the press – as the country speculated about what he might do next. The sense was unavoidable: another opportunity was coming, something bigger, more symbolic, something that could only exist in Buenos Aires. Because even at his most chaotic, Diego retained a gravitational pull. Doors opened simply because he was Diego.

A week after his brief spell at Mandiyú came to an end, Maradona was back in Buenos Aires, and speculation moved quickly. Rumours across the sports pages suggested he was close to taking over at Racing Club, one of Argentina's historic 'big five'. That talk became reality two days before Christmas, when Maradona signed his contract and Racing confirmed him as their new manager, holding the role jointly with his old assistant Carlos Fren.

His presentation in the Buenos Aires suburb of Avellaneda – complete with the now-famous floral shirt – marked the beginning of what he described as a new chapter, one that would test him from the bench rather than the pitch. Yet even then he couldn't resist hinting at a playing comeback, noting that if his suspension expired while he was still at the club, he would consider registering himself. Whether that would happen, he admitted, depended not just on the regulations but on the approval of manager Carlos Fren.

Behind the scenes, the move owed much to Claudio 'Turco' García, a Racing favourite and long-ago neighbour of Maradona in Villa Fiorito. García acted as the crucial go-between, convincing club president Juan De Stefano that the financial risk was worth taking. Maradona's limited managerial résumé mattered less than the commercial pull of his name; his arrival promised attention, sponsors and packed press conferences – benefits Racing believed would outweigh the cost of hiring the most recognisable figure in Argentine football.

In 1995, Argentine football was a city of echoes – great names and greater absences. The old titans still ruled the map: River Plate, Boca Juniors, Independiente, Racing Club, San Lorenzo. They were not just clubs but empires of devotion, each carrying the heartbeat of a *barrio*, each a flag for generations who had lived, fought and aged under their colours. Yet around them drifted ghosts – the faded banners of the sixties, the swaggering heroes of the seventies, the long shadow cast by the country's World Cup triumphs. Racing Club, once a cathedral of noise and brilliance, had become a monument to frustration. Financial ruin had bled the club dry, trophies were a memory and the cruellest part of all was to look across the street at Independiente – their eternal rival, their mirror – and see success glinting just out of reach.

To manage Racing in the mid-1990s was to step into a storm. Their fans, with a large, boisterous *barra brava* section known as *La Guardia Imperial*, were among the most passionate in Argentina, filling the Estadio Presidente Perón (the 'Cilindro') with songs, drums, banners and endless devotion. But their devotion came with desperation. They had not won the league since 1966. Each year of failure hardened into hunger, into anger, into the demand that salvation must arrive. Coaches came and went, players were hailed and discarded, but the drought endured. To step into Racing was to step into a furnace of expectation.

For Diego Maradona, who had just resigned from Deportivo Mandiyú after 12 poor games, to arrive at Racing was surreal. Just a week had passed since he stepped down from managing a small provincial club with modest aims. Now he was at one of Argentina's most historic institutions, given the keys to a giant. The announcement shocked the club's supporters and indeed, the country.

Critics who had mocked his time at Mandiyú now mocked Racing's directors for gambling on him. Supporters who adored him as a player now argued whether he could manage such a club. The press filled with headlines, caricatures, debates. And yet, once again, the absurdity made sense in Argentina's theatre of football. Who else but Diego could step from chaos into history? Who else could embody both disaster and hope?

Racing's directors, by appointing him, sought more than victories. They sought relevance, attention and the electricity of Diego's aura. They knew his record at Mandiyú was poor, but they also knew that with Diego, every game would be an event. The stadium would fill, the cameras would roll, the headlines would multiply. And in Argentine football, attention itself was currency. Still, they also hoped for miracles. Racing was desperate for trophies, desperate for pride. Could Diego, even as a rookie coach, conjure something extraordinary?

In his first match at the helm of Racing Club on 18 October 1995 against Unión de Santa Fe, the scene was already charged with tension. He stepped on to the sideline amid roaring applause, flags waving, photographers clicking away, as though a pagoda of myth had suddenly perched itself in Avellaneda. The crowd expected not just a coach but a legend in motion again – a man whose presence alone could reshape atmospheres. He wore his signature intensity from the first whistle: pacing the touchline, shouting to defenders, pulling at the shirts of forwards, always in motion, always alive in each moment of the match. That debut was not a calm entry; it was a declaration – 'I'm here again' – delivered not with quiet authority, but with the full volume of Diego's personality.

As the match wore on, Racing's frustrations grew, and the breaking point came when Unión missed a penalty that could have changed the game's course. The home crowd, already restless, erupted in whistles and jeers aimed toward the bench. Maradona, who had spent most of his career bathed in adoration, reacted in the only way his combustible personality knew: he stood up and raised both middle fingers toward the stands. It was not subtle, nor restrained – a defiant message that he would not bow to criticism, even in his new role as coach. The television cameras seized the moment, the newspapers splashed it across their front pages, and suddenly the result on the pitch was secondary. What endured was the image of Maradona, still larger than life, reminding everyone that he carried his rebellious streak into the dugout just as fiercely as he had on the field.

The job share with Fren was unconventional – officially, both carried the burden, but in reality Maradona commanded the headlines while Fren managed most of the tactical grind. It was a partnership built on loyalty more than logic. Maradona's temperamental nature and the daily pressures of management often collided, producing moments of inspiration and chaos in equal measure.

Fren has, over the years, opened up about tensions and challenges in that period. He said that their time at Racing was far more complicated than when at Mandiyú, and that turning the situation around had proven beyond what he and Diego could manage. He described a pivotal moment: after a 2–1 loss, he had apparently confronted Maradona, telling him he needed to be more '*prolijo*' (meticulous, disciplined) especially on match days, pointing out that their agreement to both wear suits had broken down when Maradona, after a domestic dispute, reportedly arrived incorrectly dressed. In later interviews, Fren had said that Maradona even shed a couple of tears, claiming it was beyond his control, and then disappeared for two or three weeks, absent from the club.

The weeks that followed passed in a haze of uneven performances – a win here, a draw there, too often followed by defeat. Racing hovered in the middle of the table, showing brief glimmers of quality that never quite took hold. The defining moment of Maradona's short tenure came during his first Avellaneda derby against Independiente, when he was sent off for squirting water at a linesman after a disputed call. Later, he brushed it off, saying he had only wanted to get the official's attention. To avoid a lengthy suspension, he paid a sizable fine and returned to the touchline. The joke was vintage Diego, but the results told a familiar story. Racing stumbled much as Mandiyú had before – still chasing a rhythm that refused to settle. A portion of the press began to wonder aloud whether it ever would.

The fans, though frustrated, continued to adore him. They sang his name, filled the Cilindro, and waved banners. For them, having Maradona as coach was both humiliation and honour. Humiliation, because results were poor. Honour, because he was Diego, the eternal number 10, the man who had lifted the World Cup. Patience would ultimately wear thin.

Behind the scenes, however, tension grew. Racing's directors demanded results. The press ridiculed his record. The players struggled to find form. Diego, proud and defiant, resisted pressure. He refused to resign, refused to apologise, refused to admit failure. He said he was building, said he needed time, said he believed in his players. But time was short, patience shorter. The defeats mounted.

And yet, even in failure, he remained a spectacle – the gravitational centre of every stadium he entered. There was no such thing as an ordinary Maradona afternoon. He barked orders from the touchline as though still playing, prowled the technical area with arms flailing, his gestures huge enough to fill the frame of every camera. When decisions went against his team, he raged at referees, veins rising in his neck, eyes blazing with that old combativeness that once terrified defenders. He insulted journalists, sparred with television pundits and used press conferences as performance spaces – theatres of defiance, grievance and charm. To his players, he was both protector and provocateur, a coach who would take the blame, absorb the heat and keep them safe within the storm he generated. He defended them not with tactics but with fire, insisting that their failures were his, their successes a collective fight.

For Argentina, this chaos was irresistible. The sight of Diego – unpredictable, magnetic, larger than life – remained intoxicating, a weekly injection of myth into the humdrum machinery of league football. Cameras followed him everywhere: every grimace, every celebration, every confrontation became headline material. Crowds came not only to watch Racing Club, but to see what Maradona would do next. He turned dugouts into stages, training grounds into tabloids, press rooms into confessionals.

For Racing's board and supporters, though, the fascination soon turned to fatigue. They needed victories, not headlines. They needed trophies, not turbulence. Maradona had given them theatre in abundance – drama, charisma, noise – but theatre does not yield points. Results lagged, frustration deepened. The club that had hoped his aura would lift them found themselves drowning in its glare. And yet, even as the defeats mounted, the stands still hummed with curiosity, because wherever Maradona went, football stopped being just a game. It became a story – unpredictable, combustible and utterly alive.

Some players thrived in the chaos. Rubén Capria, a gifted *enganche* (attacking midfielder) who previously played with Estudiantes, found freedom under Diego's permissive style. He was encouraged to dribble, to invent, to take risks. Others, particularly defenders, grew frustrated. They needed structure, organisation and clear orders. Instead, they were told to fight, to bleed, to resist. Against weaker teams, it sometimes worked. Against stronger opponents, they were overrun.

The press feasted on the drama. Every week, they filled columns not with analysis of Racing's football but with descriptions of Diego's antics. They wrote of his arguments with referees, his insults to journalists, his hugs with players, his tears in defeat. They treated each match as a performance, with Diego as protagonist. For editors, it was gold; for pundits, it was ammunition. They mocked his record, questioned his ability, doubted his future. Diego, in turn, declared war on them. He insulted commentators live on air, accused newspapers of vendettas, and reminded everyone of his playing glories. He said they would never forgive him for being

Maradona, that they hated him because he was different, because he spoke the truth. Each press conference became a theatre of conflict, each interview a duel.

Diego, for his part, refused to bow. He told the press he was building, that patience was needed, that his players would grow. He insisted he was proud of them, that they had given everything. He said results did not always reflect effort, that the referees were against him, that fate was cruel. He fought with dignity, but his words rang hollow. The defeats piled up. The pressure mounted.

In the directors' box, the mood was different. Racing's board had gambled on Diego not only for attention but for results. They had hoped his presence would inspire players, intimidate rivals and change fortunes. Instead, they watched their team stumble through mediocrity, drifting far from contention, humiliated in the *clásico* against Independiente, unable to build momentum. They faced not salvation but another season of disappointment. Their patience frayed. They saw in Diego not a solution but a problem, not a saviour but a distraction. The press mocked them as fools, saying they had hired a showman instead of a strategist, a name instead of a coach. Their pride, their credibility, was at stake.

The game was up for Maradona and Racing. His record was poor: 11 matches, two wins, six draws, three defeats. A better win ratio than at his previous club. Not catastrophic, but certainly nowhere near enough for Racing. Diego left the club after just 79 days, another coach in Racing's long list of failed saviours. The press reported it with glee, mocking him, dissecting his failures, questioning his future. Diego, wounded, raged. He said he had been betrayed, that he had been given no time, that his players had fought bravely. He walked away defiant, as always, his pride intact, his myth undimmed.

But if Racing ended in bitterness, it was also a prelude. Maradona's first two experiments in management – at Mandiyú and then in Avellaneda – had shown him the unforgiving glare of the dugout, where his name alone could not guarantee results. For the press, these failures were ammunition; for Diego, they were scars that hardened his defiance. He stepped back from coaching, retreating once more into the tumult of his personal life, his health and the endless scrutiny that followed him. Yet even in failure, the myth of Maradona only grew. He had walked away bruised but not broken, a fallen idol who refused to bow, a man whose second acts were always only the prelude to another comeback.

The press met his dismissal with a kind of gleeful inevitability. Headlines dripped with ridicule, dissecting his record of two wins in 11 games and branding the experiment a failure. Columns mocked the mismatch between his charisma and his results, insisting that celebrity had once again trumped substance. For many journalists, his managerial career was finished before it had properly begun.

Among Racing supporters, the reaction was far more complex. Some sang his name one last time, holding banners of thanks for the man who had once lifted Argentina to a World Cup. They said that even without silverware, he had brought their club a fleeting sense of significance. Yet others were far less forgiving. To many within Avellaneda's fanbase, his spell in the dugout remains a chapter best forgotten – a reminder that even national icons can falter when passion outpaces preparation.

In the years that followed, Carlos Fren spoke of Racing with the unease of a man still haunted by unfinished business. He had been Diego Maradona's right-hand man, his confidant, his translator in the strange new language of management. Yet time turned that partnership sour. Fren would later describe a deep sense of betrayal, the feeling that Maradona had failed him – not only as a colleague but as a friend. Money was part of it, but not all of it. There was also pride, bruised trust and the heartbreak of seeing a shared dream collapse in public. What had begun as a chance for redemption – for both men – ended as another reminder that the world of Argentine football devours its own. Fren had imagined the two of them as equals on the touchline, guiding Racing out of the shadows. Instead, he was left to tell the story years later, his voice thick with regret, still searching for the version of events that might make peace with what happened.

Racing itself offered little in the way of solace. It became a vivid, combustible chapter in Maradona's long drama – another act in a life that refused to run to script. Without the ball at his feet, he was exposed to the merciless logic of coaching: systems, structures, discipline, accountability. Gone was the player who could settle arguments with a flick of his left boot. In his place stood a man wrestling with egos, finances and his own restlessness. Still, even stripped of magic, Maradona could not avoid spectacle. Every matchday had a sense of a walk into the unknown – the dugout, his stage, the cameras, his audience, the country leaning in to see what he'd do next.

His spell in Avellaneda lasted only a handful of months, but it carried the same fierce energy that followed him everywhere: brilliance laced with chaos, loyalty tinged with betrayal, hope collapsing into heartbreak. When it ended, nothing had really been solved – not for Racing, not for Fren and certainly not for Diego. Yet, as always, he left behind noise, colour and stories that would never fade. In the messy poetry of Maradona's life, even failure burned brightly.

He would return to playing one last time and at a club he knew so very well.

CHAPTER TWO

The Last Dance in Blue and Gold

BY 1995, Diego Maradona was no longer the street prodigy from Villa Fiorito, nor the divine genius who had conquered the world in 1986, nor even the battered idol who had ruled Naples. He was a man who had stared down his own mortality more than once, been banned from football for drugs, hounded by scandal and chased by his own legend. His body carried the receipts of excess – knees shredded by years of collisions, a heart strained by the chaos that never left him. At the age of 35, many thought the story was over, that the curtain had finally fallen. Yet Argentina is a country that lives on the possibility of resurrection, and with Diego, that faith burned brighter than reason. So when rumours began to drift through Buenos Aires that he might return to Boca Juniors – his first great love, his cathedral, the place where the myth began – the city stirred. On the streets, in cafés, in the terraces of La Bombonera, people waited, sensing that what was potentially coming was not merely a comeback, but a second birth.

Maradona first proposed returning to Boca Juniors as both player and coach, but the club's leadership, headed by president Antonio Alegre, hesitated. Boca's finances were strained and meeting Diego's salary demands seemed impossible. Then came the intervention that changed everything: a group of businessmen, among them media magnate Eduardo Eurnekian, stepped in to broker his return. The public clamour was undeniable – Argentina longed to see Maradona back where he belonged, on the pitch. Every club in the country would have welcomed him, but it was Boca Juniors – his spiritual home – that would be blessed with the honour of handing him the number 10 shirt once more. Destiny, it seemed, was calling. Eventually, Maradona agreed to return solely as a player, setting the stage for one of football's most anticipated comebacks.

After his turbulent managerial stint with Racing alongside Carlos Fren, Diego had thrown himself into training, preparing for the expiration of his 15-month ban from playing. He wanted to feel the grass beneath his boots again, to reclaim the game that had always been his true home. He still believed he had something to give – and the country, weary yet hopeful, believed it too.

That belief erupted into reality on Sunday, 7 October 1995, when Diego Armando Maradona stepped on to the pitch at La Bombonera as a Boca Juniors player for the first time in 13 years. The stadium was already quaking before he arrived. From the street outside – Brandsen – came the roar of tens of thousands, a sound like surf breaking against stone. Flags rippled from balconies, blue and gold smoke drifted above the rooftops and the entire neighbourhood seemed to tilt toward the stadium, drawn to the return of its native son.

His return to competitive play in the Argentine Primera División was met with enormous anticipation. Maradona – now sporting a bleached blonde streak in his hair and a goatee beard – led the Xeneize out to a 1–0 victory over Colón. At the end of the match, a feisty Maradona invited Colón midfielder Julio Toresani for a fist fight. Not on the pitch, but outside his house, on the corner of Habana and Segurola streets, where Diego lived in those days. Toresani declined. Maradona was selected for a 'random' drug test at the final whistle.

The following week, Boca faced Argentinos Juniors at Vélez Sarsfield's ground. Argentinos had given the young Diego his start in professional football, so when the number 10 scored a free kick, 20 minutes from time, he respectfully declined to celebrate.

One of the matches Maradona was most looking forward to was the *Superclásico*, arguably one of the most famous fixtures in world football – River Plate against Boca Juniors – at the Monumental on 26 November. He and his family had long been Boca fans, even before he was a player, so a goal against River during his triumphant return would be the icing on the cake. It wasn't to be, as the game played out as a 0–0 draw, but Boca still maintained their unbeaten run. At the final whistle, dozens of journalists, photographers and television cameramen surrounded the 35-year-old genius.

His first games back were treated like national holidays. On matchdays the streets of La Boca, the working-class neighbourhood where the famous La Bombonera stadium stood, felt like a party: Diego Maradona will be playing here today. Crowds swelled, journalists filled columns with tributes, cameras followed his every step. Every time he touched the ball, a gasp ran through the stands. Every dribble, every feint, even if slower than before, carried the weight of memory. He was no longer the fastest, no longer unstoppable, but he was still Diego, and Diego's mere presence was magic. The television commentators spoke not of tactics but of emotion. They described his movements with reverence, as though narrating a sacred ritual. For a country battered by economic troubles and political uncertainty, his return was a balm, a reminder that joy could still exist.

On the pitch, his role shifted. He was no longer the young engine who drove attacks relentlessly, but a wise old general, dictating rhythm with his left foot, guiding younger team-mates, offering flashes of brilliance that reminded everyone of who he had been. He played with intelligence, with vision. He may not have run as before, but he still saw the game as no one else could. His passes split defences, his free kicks bent toward goal with uncanny accuracy, his presence alone drew opponents and created space for others. Boca's younger players spoke of the awe of sharing the field with him, of learning from his whispers, of feeling his hand on their shoulders. For them, it was like playing under a living monument.

Off the pitch, his presence transformed the atmosphere of Argentine football. Stadiums that normally revelled in booing Boca now erupted into chants of Diego's name when he appeared. Rivals who had once loathed him bowed their heads in respect. Every away match became a festival of tributes, a chance for fans to say they had seen Maradona one last time. It was as though the entire country knew this was not about league tables or titles but about history. They wanted to witness him, to embrace him, to participate in the last dance.

La Bombonera became something more than a stadium; it turned into a place of worship. The concrete shook beneath the weight of it all – the drums, the chanting, the crack of fireworks stitched into the night air. Banners were unfurled across the terraces, Diego rendered as deity, saint, talisman. Children pulled on the number 10 shirt as if it were a rite of passage. Old men wiped their eyes, carried back to the afternoons when he first bent the laws of gravity and good sense. Each generation found its own meaning in his return: for some, a memory recovered; for others, an introduction. For everyone, though, it was the same thing – devotion.

The press, always hungry for drama, chronicled his every gesture. They wrote of his embraces with fans, his fiery words in press conferences, his jokes with teammates. They analysed his weight, his fitness, his moods. Every detail became national news. When he played well, headlines shouted of the return of genius. When he played poorly, they still wrote of his courage, his will, his refusal to surrender. Diego could not escape the microscope, but he also did not want to. He lived for the spectacle, for the attention, for the chance to remain at the centre of the world. In his first year back at Boca, he scored five times in 24 games.

As time passed, Maradona's long struggle with addiction began to resurface, and he spoke openly about it, confronting the reality rather than hiding from it. In an interview with the Argentine magazine *Gente*, he admitted that his battle with drugs was not something that simply ended – it was a lifelong fight. That same August, determined to regain control, he travelled to Switzerland and checked into the Bellelay Clinic, a rehabilitation centre known for its discretion and intensive treatment programmes. He said he wanted to recover not only for himself but for his two young daughters, who remained at the centre of his efforts to rebuild his life. The clinic had been recommended by a close friend, and Diego chose it after confessing that he no longer trusted the quality or sincerity of treatment available back home in Argentina.

Even as he sought treatment, the world – and especially Argentina – watched with a mix of hope and unease. The media followed his recovery like a national drama: every clinic visit filmed, every step scrutinised, every relapse feared. For millions of fans, it was heartbreaking to see their idol, once invincible, brought so low. Yet beneath the noise, there was also a collective wish – that Diego might somehow find peace, that he could conquer the same demons that had chased him for years. The same intensity that once fuelled his brilliance now powered a relentless struggle between destruction and redemption. His stay at the clinic, however, lasted only ten days.

When he was back at home, his health continued to falter. By April 1997 he was hospitalised after a sudden spike in his blood pressure during a television appearance in Chile, a stark reminder that years of excess had left his body vulnerable. And yet, Diego refused to accept decline. By mid-1997 he was back with Boca, insisting he still had the strength to compete. His return was an act of defiance, a last attempt to show that he could still command the stage, even as whispers of relapse and doubts from the club's directors hung heavily in the background. His team-mates rallied around him. They spoke of his leadership, his charisma, his endless love for the game. They said that even when he was not at his best, his belief inspired them. Coaches built teams around his diminished role, not because of tactics but because of what he represented. No one wanted to bench Diego. No one wanted to tell him 'no'. For many, he was bigger than the sport itself.

And Diego himself seemed to thrive on love. He smiled more, he laughed, he embraced fans, he kissed the badge. He knew his body was failing, but he refused to let it silence him. He wanted to give everything he had left to Boca, to Argentina, to the people who had never abandoned him. Every match was an act of gratitude, a gift. He may not have been the Diego of 1986, but he was still Diego, and that was enough.

The younger members of the Boca squad looked at him as a living monument. Players like Martín Palermo, who would later become a club idol in his own right, remembered what it meant to share the pitch with Diego. He said that even when he struggled, his aura transformed the game. Opponents marked him tightly, even if his body no longer threatened them, because his reputation still did. Referees treated him with deference. Fans roared every time he touched the ball. He remained, in every sense, the centre of attention.

On 25 October 1997, the Monumental – usually River Plate's fortress – became the stage for one of football's quietest farewells. Boca Juniors snatched a 2–1 victory over their arch rivals. Maradona, visibly diminished in physique and stamina, started the match, but at half-time he was substituted. The young Juan Román Riquelme came on in his place – an almost symbolic passing of the torch. That would be the final 45 minutes of professional football that Diego Armando Maradona ever played. His career, threaded through with brilliance and contradiction, ended not with a flourish but with a substitution.

The reason soon became clear: Maradona had tested positive for a banned substance following a recent match, a revelation that sent shockwaves through Argentine football. He insisted on his innocence, suggesting the sample may have been contaminated or mishandled, but the damage was irreversible. The timing added a cruel symmetry – on his 37th birthday, 30 October 1997, he announced his retirement from professional football, saying the moment had come to walk away for good. For Argentina, and for the wider world, it felt like a curtain closing on something irreplaceable. His career – chaotic, radiant, and unforgettable – ended as it had begun: dramatically, on his own terms.

CHAPTER THREE

The Game Without the Ball

THE LIGHTS in the studio burned white against the dark. Outside, Buenos Aires was sliding into evening, the city humming with its usual noise – buses, radios, distant fireworks – but inside, everything was still. A microphone waited on a plain wooden table. Diego adjusted the collar of his shirt, glanced at the floor and took a slow breath. For once, there were no team-mates, no crowd, no ball at his feet – only the echo of his own name.

In the days after his retirement announcement, Maradona faced the cameras one final time as a professional footballer, though few could yet imagine him as anything else. His voice wavered as he confessed that the player within him had reached the end, and that no one felt the pain of that truth more deeply than he did. For once, the bravado slipped, revealing not the global icon but a man mourning the loss of himself. Football had been more than his profession – it had been his language, his faith, his pulse, the force that gave his life coherence. Now, with the stadium lights dimmed and the roar of the crowd fading, he looked momentarily lost, as if unsure how to exist without the game that had both made and consumed him. It was a rare, fragile silence from a man who had spent a lifetime shouting at the world.

He also revealed that he had made a promise to his father: that if his name was ever again linked to drugs, he would walk away for good. The test result, damning and inescapable, left him no choice but to keep that promise. It was a gesture that carried both pride and pain – the obedience of a son and the resignation of a fallen idol. For once, he did not rage against the world. He simply surrendered.

But withdrawal was not in Maradona's nature. In the weeks and months that followed, he tried, with uneven discipline, to manage his health and addiction. Doctors and clinics in Buenos Aires alternated between hope and despair. He went through detox programmes, emerging thinner and quieter, only to relapse into the chaotic rhythm that had long defined his off-field life. Cocaine, alcohol, late nights, overeating – each addiction seemed to replace another. And yet, through it all, he retained an almost mythic energy, as though the same force that had driven him past defenders now refused to let him rest.

Instead of vanishing from public life, Diego reinvented his role. If he could no longer play, he could still *perform*. In early 1998, Maradona remained anything but silent. Though he had announced his retirement, he immediately shifted roles, briefly exploring a comeback with lower-division side All Boys before ultimately rejecting the idea and staying retired. He began appearing as a television commentator for the France '98 World Cup, although legal troubles and a suspended sentence from a 1994 air-rifle incident delayed his travel to France.

Despite being well into his late 30s and retired, he publicly admitted his disappointment at being unable to participate in the tournament as a player, calling himself 'depressed' at the exclusion, before defending his infamous 1986 'Hand of God' goal to the press, telling them that he would use the tactic 'against any team in the world'.

Though he was now a TV pundit, and not part of Argentina's squad, Maradona remained central to their narrative. His presence in media coverage ensured that every misstep, every tactical debate, every moment of Argentine pain or joy was filtered through his voice. The contrast between his physical absence and his magnetic presence only deepened the mythology: Maradona was no longer the player writing history, but the commentator shaping how that history would be remembered.

The 1998 World Cup arrived as both a promise and a provocation for Argentina. It was their first major tournament without Diego Armando Maradona in any capacity – no number 10 on the field, no captain's armband, no divine mischief guiding them through impossible matches. The team was in the hands of Daniel Passarella, the stern disciplinarian who had once been Diego's team-mate and later his antagonist.

Their relationship had always been combustible: two proud men, both icons of Argentina's footballing psyche, forever divided by ego and ideology. Passarella represented order, fitness, military precision; Maradona, rebellion, improvisation, poetry. For many Argentines, it was hard not to see the 1998 tournament as a test of whether the nation could thrive without its chaotic genius.

And yet, on paper, Argentina were formidable. The team brimmed with talent: Gabriel Batistuta, a ruthless striker whose goals seemed to explode from his boot; Ariel Ortega, the young playmaker with that low centre of gravity and a hint of Diego's swagger in his dribble; Claudio López, Javier Zanetti, Juan Sebastián Verón and a defence disciplined enough to withstand storms. Passarella had drilled them into shape: short hair, strict diets, a sense of military unity. The team entered France in confident rhythm. They advanced through the group stages with a 1–0 win over Japan, a 5–0 demolition of Jamaica – Batistuta scoring a hat-trick that reminded fans of the days when Argentina's number 9 had the power of a cannon – and a tense, professional victory over Croatia.

By the time they reached the round of 16, Argentina had rediscovered something of their old selves: pride mixed with paranoia, artistry fused with aggression. Fate, always a dramatist, handed them England. The pairing instantly rekindled the ghost of 1986 – Maradona's 'Hand of God,' his 'Goal of the Century' and that sense that Argentina's footballing identity had been written in those moments of divine contradiction. The build-up to the 1998 clash was drenched in nostalgia and nationalism. British papers spoke of revenge, Argentine ones spoke of heritage. And Maradona could not resist weighing in as he watched the match on television. He reminded anyone who called him that Argentina's legend had been built 'on our feet, on our heart, against them'.

The match in Saint-Étienne was electric from the start. Ortega weaved through the English midfield with that jittery brilliance that evoked Diego's old ghost. Batistuta converted an early penalty, only for Alan Shearer to respond in kind moments later. Then came Michael Owen's stunning solo goal – a teenage flash of genius that even Maradona reportedly admired. But Argentina refused to bow. Javier Zanetti equalised from a clever Ortega free kick, restoring the rhythm of destiny. Extra time couldn't separate them; penalties loomed. Argentina's shootout, cold and precise, broke English hearts once more. The victory sent Buenos Aires into delirium. Cars honked through the night, flags waved from balconies and the chant of 'Argentina! Argentina!' rolled through the winter air. It wasn't 1986, but it felt close enough to taste.

Maradona oscillated between pride and possessiveness. He praised Batistuta's ruthlessness, called Ortega 'a crack' – a common phrase in Spanish for someone to be admired – and congratulated the team. He liked to remind people that the Argentina the world had learned to fear – the real Argentina – had been born in his time. That shirt, he would say, still carried his sweat, its fabric steeped in his history. Watching from the sidelines was torment, like seeing someone else act out a role he had written for himself.

The dream, however, began to unravel in the quarter-finals in Marseille. Argentina met the Netherlands in a match that was tight, tactical, beautiful and cruel. Both sides traded blows: Ortega was sent off for head-butting Dutch keeper Edwin van der Sar, Batistuta hit the post, and the clock bled toward extra time. Then, in the 89th minute, Dennis Bergkamp produced a goal that seemed to defy reason – cushioning a 40-yard pass out of the sky, slicing inside, and finishing past Carlos Roa in a single, graceful movement. It was football distilled into art, and it destroyed Argentina's hopes in an instant.

Maradona, watching that goal in the TV studio, fell into silence. He recognised brilliance instantly, even when it came wearing the wrong colours. That night was football at its most cruel – one flash of beauty and everything was over. The defeat carried a sting that went beyond the scoreboard. Argentina had fallen, but deeper still was the realisation that the game was evolving, discovering new heroes, new conjurers of wonder. For a man who had once embodied the very essence of footballing magic, it was like watching the world turn a page without him. Yet the past refused to vanish. The echoes of 1986 still reverberated and Maradona's shadow stretched across every match Argentina played. Whether they triumphed or stumbled, he lingered at the edges – a permanent presence, a reminder of a standard that could never quite be matched.

For Maradona, the tournament was heartbreak. He had once been the architect of Argentina's greatest triumph; now he was reduced to a commentator, railing at coaches, praising players he admired and lamenting decisions he despised. Even in retirement, his words carried weight. In France '98, Diego was not the player writing history, but the voice ensuring that history could not be told without him.

When he retired from football, he did not retire from life. TV punditry was one thing, but Diego always wanted that something more. For men like him, life itself is a stadium, an endless game played in front of millions, a match where every gesture is magnified and every stumble analysed. He was absolutely incapable of anonymity. His shadow was too large, his myth far too vast. And so, in the years that followed his playing career, he plunged into a new stage of existence, one marked by health crises that nearly killed him, by political friendships that astonished the world, by exile in Cuba under the protection of Fidel Castro, and by one of the most surreal reinventions in television history. These were the years when Diego no longer played football, but somehow played life with the same reckless, intoxicating style.

What came next was less a retirement than a transformation. Stripped of the jersey but not the stage, Maradona became a kind of performance in himself – a living contradiction who blurred the line between man and myth. Fame, which had once been a consequence of his genius, now became his oxygen. He appeared on talk shows, fronted commercials and held impromptu press conferences that felt more like theatre than journalism. His opinions – on football, politics, fame, even religion – were delivered with the same intensity as his old dribbles through England's defence. He was no longer scoring goals but provoking reactions, commanding attention through sheer force of personality. In Argentina, he remained an unavoidable presence: loved, loathed, but never ignored. The game might have ended for him, but the performance of being Maradona had only just begun.

By the end of the 1990s, he was a man trying to stitch his legend back together. The roar of the crowd had faded, the boots were hung up and what remained was the echo – an echo of adoration, scandal and self-destruction. He was by now heavier, slower and trapped in a cycle of hospital visits and television appearances that turned his once-private chaos into public entertainment. The footballing god of Mexico '86 had become the man shaking his fist at cameras, a walking headline. Yet beneath the noise, Diego was brooding on something larger – a way to reclaim the story that had been told about him by everyone else.

By 1999, he was determined to seize control of his own legend. Argentina's gossip pages treated him like a soap opera character, while European journalists chronicled his downfall with grim fascination. Maradona, never one to accept the role of villain or victim, decided to write his own version of events. He teamed up with Daniel Arcucci, the journalist who had followed him since the early '80s, and Ernesto Cherquis Bialo, one of Argentina's most respected editors. Together they began shaping hours of conversation into something that was neither apology nor boast, but an act of possession. Diego didn't want to be explained – he wanted to be *heard*.

CHAPTER FOUR

The God and the Comandante

THE NEWSSTANDS of Buenos Aires were drowning in his face again. Stacks of glossy magazines, posters, papers – all the same headline: 'Maradona speaks'. Outside cafés, people argued about what he'd say this time. On television, his voice crackled from interviews recorded in Havana – where he was now spending increasing amounts of time – his accent still pure Villa Fiorito but slowed by age and recovery. The city that once wept for him now waited to hear him explain himself. After years of silence, the fallen idol had found a new way to perform – not with a ball, but with words.

When Maradona's autobiography, *Yo soy el Diego* appeared in 2000, it landed like a shockwave. The title alone carried defiance – a declaration that he remained *El Diez*, even if his body had begun to betray him. Copies vanished from Buenos Aires shelves within days and spread through Latin America like contraband faith. In Naples, bookshops set it in their windows as if it were a holy text. Critics were unsure what to make of it but couldn't look away. Some saw confession without regret; others a man locked in battle with his own myth. Readers devoured it for the same reason they had always watched him – because Diego never pretended to be like anyone else. The book wasn't neat or polished; it was a tangle of ego, nostalgia and uneasy truth. It was Maradona distilled – chaotic, irresistible and unmistakably his.

For Diego himself, the autobiography was therapy. It allowed him to reclaim his narrative, to tell his story in his own words rather than through the lens of the press. He wrote of his pain, his struggles, his love for the ball, his sense of betrayal by institutions, his endless connection to the people and the family that he loved so much. The tone was intimate and combative, vulnerable and proud. Readers felt they were hearing Diego himself, sitting in a café, telling stories, swearing, laughing, crying. It was raw, unpolished, but authentic – and that authenticity was what made it powerful.

By the turn of the millennium, Maradona's body was no longer merely exhausted – it was in open revolt. Decades of excess, cocaine, alcohol, overeating and emotional turbulence had finally cornered him. The warning signs had long been there: the breathlessness during training sessions, the bloated face, the irregular appearances on television where his voice trembled and his eyes burned with restless energy. He had always lived as though indestructible, as though the sheer force of will that once carried him past defenders could also outmanoeuvre mortality itself. But in January 2000, that illusion collapsed spectacularly.

He was on holiday in Punta del Este, Uruguay – a resort town known for its glamour and casinos – when the crisis struck. Late one night, after what reports later described as a cocaine binge, he suffered a massive cardiac event. He collapsed in his hotel suite, his body convulsing, his heart faltering. The ambulance arrived within minutes, but by then the panic had spread. News of his hospitalisation broke before dawn, and by morning Argentina was in collective shock. Television channels abandoned their programming to broadcast live from the hospital gates. Newspapers printed emergency editions. The familiar image of Diego – that mischievous grin, that boyish exuberance – was replaced by footage of doctors grimly briefing reporters. They spoke of arrhythmia, of severe heart failure, of the fragility of his condition. The word 'death' was whispered, then spoken aloud.

Outside the hospital, a small handful of fans gathered in vigil. Some brought flags, others brought rosaries. They sang his name: 'Olé, olé, olé, olé … Diego, Diego!' Back in Buenos Aires, the story led front pages and evening news programmes, many framing it as yet another 'long night'. The public reaction, though varied in tone, shared a common anxiety: for the first time, the fear was not disciplinary nor sporting but existential – the sense that the greatest player Argentina had produced might now be fighting for his life.

Inside the intensive care unit, doctors worked to stabilise him. He was sedated, monitored, and tethered to machines that breathed when he could not. Days passed in tense uncertainty. Every minor improvement was celebrated as a national event; every setback triggered fresh waves of dread. For nearly a week, the country lived between bulletins. Then, slowly, Diego began to recover. Against odds that seemed impossible, he clawed his way back from the edge, just as he had done so many times on the pitch. It was as though his body, however damaged, retained that same obstinate refusal to surrender that had defined his career.

When Maradona finally left the hospital – weakened, pale, but out of danger – the conversation shifted from shock to something more existential: how could he survive his own excesses? The answer, improbably, pointed toward Havana.

His relationship with Fidel Castro was one of the unlikeliest in modern sport, yet somehow it made sense. Both men operated at a mythic scale, shaped by hardship and celebrated by those who saw in them a voice against power. Castro admired Maradona's brilliance and his instinctive rebellion; Maradona, in turn, was drawn to the Cuban leader's revolutionary aura and his defiance of the United States. Their connection dated back to the 1980s, when Maradona's fame had begun to spill far beyond football and Castro recognised in him not just an athlete, but a symbol – a prodigious, unruly son of the working class whose story resonated across Latin America.

Castro, long an admirer of Maradona and already familiar with his struggles, extended an invitation for him to continue his treatment and rehabilitation in

Cuba. It was a gesture that blended politics, personal regard and the Cuban leader's habit of taking interest in figures he considered emblematic. For Maradona, the offer represented more than a change of medical setting. Argentina, with its relentless scrutiny and constant reminders of his decline, felt suffocating. Cuba, by contrast, promised distance, privacy and the protection of a leader he openly revered. It was the beginning of a chapter in which recovery, exile and friendship became inseparable.

Diego arrived in Havana on Wednesday, 19 January 2000, after a brief stop in Holguín on Cuba's eastern coast. A local media frenzy greeted him in the arrivals hall, where he revealed a fresh tattoo of Che Guevara on his right arm. His speech was noticeably slurred, but he carried himself with defiance, flanked by his wife, his mother and his business manager Guillermo Coppola. He spoke of wanting to organise an exhibition match as a gesture of thanks to the Cuban people for their welcome.

The reception, however, was not unanimously affectionate. Amid the noise and cameras, an Argentinian tourist denounced him as a poor example for the young people who idolised him. Irritated, Maradona brushed off the remark with a hint of disbelief and continued toward the car waiting to collect his entourage. It was an unusual moment: he was not accustomed to being publicly rebuked by his own countrymen outside the confines of a football stadium, and the interruption clearly struck a nerve.

In the days that followed, Cuban officials and medical staff took immediate charge of his care. He was ushered straight to a private clinic on the outskirts of Havana, where his rehabilitation would begin. Castro visited him soon after, walking through the corridors with the slow, deliberate confidence that had long defined him. The two spent hours together, drinking coffee and smoking cigars – a striking contradiction for a patient recovering from heart complications, but one that neither seemed inclined to acknowledge.

Their bond deepened quickly. Castro viewed Maradona as a kind of prodigal son of Latin America, a gifted yet wayward figure whose brilliance and volatility reflected many of the region's own contradictions. Maradona, in turn, saw in Castro a paternal presence – protective, authoritative and understanding of what it meant to live at the extremes of adoration and controversy. He later described Castro's welcome as warm and instinctively caring, as though he were embracing someone he had long felt responsible for.

While in Cuba, he entered rehabilitation, alternating between medical treatment and long conversations with Fidel about sport, politics and destiny. The state offered him privacy, the public offered him worship, and for a time, he seemed to find balance. He trained lightly, swam, played pick-up games with children and even began to write. But even in this Caribbean exile, Diego could never fully escape himself. The contradictions that defined him – discipline and indulgence, repentance and rebellion – remained. Yet Havana gave him what Buenos Aires never could: stillness.

For the first time in years, Diego's survival did not seem miraculous but possible. Under Fidel's watchful gaze, he began to rebuild – physically, spiritually and symbolically. What began as a medical exile would evolve into one of the most emblematic friendships of his later life, shaping not only his politics but his sense of identity. The myth of Maradona – the man who cheated death, defied authority and found refuge with a revolutionary – entered a new phase.

Diego was alive, for now, and in Havana the world's most volatile footballer became its most improbable patient, cradled by a nation that saw in him both its struggle and its soul.

Maradona spent his Cuban years moving between state-provided houses, travelling across Havana in ageing cars and attracting attention wherever he appeared. His time on the island was a mixture of rehabilitation, therapy and, at times, renewed excess. The clinics worked to pull him away from addiction, yet relapses still occurred. His weight swung dramatically; he later underwent gastric bypass surgery, shedding dozens of kilos and altering his appearance to such a degree that at moments he seemed reborn. But the transformation never held steady. There were periods when he looked revitalised and almost youthful, and others when he appeared swollen, unwell and depleted.

Maradona's years in Cuba left marks that emerged much later, and the disclosures in his final phase added new complexity to an already intricate personal story. In 2019, his lawyer announced that Maradona would legally recognise three children born during his time on the island. The identities and backgrounds of those children were not publicly detailed and the information released was limited, but the announcement expanded the number of his acknowledged offspring and drew renewed attention to the private life he led during his long periods of rehabilitation in Havana.

This was not the first time questions of paternity had shaped Maradona's public life. During his Napoli years, he had fathered a son, Diego Maradona Jr., born in 1986. Maradona initially rejected the claim, but after a protracted legal process, an Italian court formally established paternity in 1993. Their personal relationship evolved only gradually. The two finally met in 2003 during a golf tournament in Fiuggi, a cautious first encounter that opened the door to a slow reconciliation. Over the following decade the connection deepened, and in 2016 – in a moment widely covered by Argentine and Italian media – Maradona embraced his son publicly and spoke with unusual openness, telling reporters that he loved him and that he saw so much of himself in Junior.

Another chapter unfolded in Argentina in the 1990s, when his relationship with Valeria Sabalain resulted in the birth of a daughter, Jana. Again, there were years of contention and legal steps before Maradona acknowledged her publicly in 2014. Their bond strengthened over time, and she later spent extended periods living with him, including during his Dubai period many years later.

Later, during his relationship with Verónica Ojeda, Maradona became the father of Diego Fernando, whose birth was publicly confirmed and widely covered in Argentine media. Taken together, these episodes reveal a pattern that shaped much of Maradona's personal life: delayed recognitions, legal processes, emotional reconciliations, and an evolving sense of responsibility. The Cuban revelations in 2019 formed part of that broader story. They did not so much expose a hidden truth as underline the contradictions of a man who lived intensely, who struggled with intimacy as much as he sought it, and who, in his later years, appeared increasingly intent on repairing the fractures of his past.

As the years in Cuba unfolded at the turn of the millennium, Diego slowly recovered stability. His health improved after surgeries, his addictions lessened under medical supervision, his weight dropped. He began to look more like himself again, though older, scarred, marked by decades of excess. He gave interviews about his life, about his love for his two daughters with his wife Claudia Villafañe, about his pride in his career. He spoke of wanting to coach again, to return to football, to give back to the game that had given him everything. Argentina listened, half-hopeful, half-sceptical. Could he truly return? Could he truly change? With Diego, nothing was impossible, but absolutely nothing was certain.

The years following Maradona's retirement were anything but settled. They unfolded in bursts of crisis and recovery, moments of clarity followed by chaos. He moved between hospital wards, television studios and political stages, spending long periods in treatment and rehabilitation in Cuba. He was alive, but adrift – cut loose from the rhythm that had once defined him. The roar of the terraces had fallen silent, replaced by the uneasy stillness of a fame without direction. His final appearance as a player – a half-time substitution against River Plate in 1997 – had not been the grand farewell many had imagined. It had been an ending without ceremony, abrupt and unfinished. For a nation that sanctifies its heroes through spectacle, Argentina had been denied the closure it craved: a final act worthy of the man who had once seemed larger than the game itself.

Four years passed in that void – years in which Maradona's name never left the headlines, though rarely for footballing reasons. But time, and perhaps contrition, began to smooth the edges of resentment. By 2001, a new idea had taken root among the Boca hierarchy and the Argentine Football Association: Diego deserved a farewell that matched his myth. He had been denied closure on the pitch, so they would give him a stage worthy of his legend. Plans were drawn, tickets vanished instantly, television networks cleared their schedules. It would be more than a testimonial; it would be a pilgrimage. And when the date was set, La Bombonera itself began to stir – the old stadium preparing, at last, to welcome home and say a farewell to its greatest son.

It was 10 November 2001, and La Bombonera had begun to fill hours before kick-off. By evening the stadium was heaving, terraces packed with tens of thousands of supporters waving flags, hoisting banners and wearing the number 10 shirt one last time. Outside, the narrow streets of La Boca were gridlocked with fans who had no tickets but refused to be anywhere else. This wasn't merely a testimonial; it was a national celebration, a mass farewell. The atmosphere evoked the night of his 1995 return, but now carried a greater weight. Everyone understood that this was the final time Diego Maradona would step on to a pitch as a player.

The match, officially Argentina versus a Rest of the World XI, became almost secondary to the occasion. The visiting side featured a remarkable cast – the likes of Hristo Stoichkov, Enzo Francescoli, Carlos Valderrama, René Higuita, Davor Šuker, Iván Córdoba and Carlos Gamarra – but all eyes were on Maradona. He captained the Argentine team, scored twice from the penalty spot and absorbed the kind of ovation few athletes ever receive. The noise was constant and overwhelming: chants, tears, applause, a stadium roaring its thanks. Some supporters wept, others sang themselves hoarse, entire families clung to one another. For a night, Argentina didn't just honour a footballer; it collectively saluted a life that had shaped its identity.

Maradona himself was overcome. He waved to the stands, kissed the turf, embraced team-mates, laughed, cried, raised his arms. His parents, his daughters and his whole family were there for the affair. He was not the lean genius of 1986; he was older, heavier, slower. But none of that mattered. He was there, on the grass of La Bombonera, wearing the colours of Boca Juniors, receiving the ovation of a lifetime. For him, it was redemption. For Argentina, it was closure.

During the match, he showed flashes of his old self. A clever dribble, a precise pass, a smile after a cheeky feint. Every touch was met with roars. When he scored from the penalty spot, the stadium erupted as though it were a World Cup Final. The goals themselves were simple, but the symbolism was immense. Diego Armando Maradona had scored at La Bombonera for the last time. He raised his arms and wept openly. For fans, it was perfect.

The most unforgettable moment of the night came after the final whistle, when Maradona stepped forward to address the crowd. His voice was strained with emotion, the delivery uneven and raw, but unmistakably sincere. He spoke of gratitude – for the devotion of the supporters, for their loyalty through triumphs and failures, for the forgiveness they had shown him across the years. He then articulated a reflection that would become one of the defining lines of his legacy: the idea that, despite everything he had done wrong in his personal life, the game itself remained untarnished. He acknowledged his own flaws and excesses, but insisted that football – the ball, the essence of the sport – was pure, untouched by human chaos. It was both an admission and a kind of self-absolution. He also defended the work he had put into his career, pushing back against those who claimed he had been handed everything, making clear that nothing in his life had come easily. He was mortal, but the game was eternal. And he had been its chosen prophet.

CHAPTER FIVE

A Gospel According to Maradona

THE WORLD Cup had returned, and Diego had returned to the confines of the television studio. In Seoul and Sapporo, the lights blazed, the anthems rang and the cameras searched the stands for him out of habit – as if the tournament still needed his shadow to feel complete. He sat behind a desk covered in papers and coffee cups, headset crooked, eyes alive with the same ferocity that once terrified defenders. The war was over, but the commentary had just begun.

During the 2002 World Cup, Maradona split his time between Canal 13 and *La Nación*, serving as both commentator and provocateur. From the studio, he spoke with the same volatility that once electrified the pitch. He railed against FIFA and its president, accusing them of greed and hypocrisy, claiming the game's guardians had long since sold its soul. When Argentina crashed out early under Marcelo Bielsa, his fury shifted homeward. He lamented a team that, in his eyes, had lost its imagination and conviction, a side that no longer carried the fire of his generation. His remarks filled newspapers and broadcasts across the continent – Diego once again the nation's loudest, most unfiltered conscience.

That same year, his health continued to deteriorate. He was hospitalised several times in Uruguay and Cuba for hypertension, arrhythmia and issues linked to his long history of drug addiction. His weight had ballooned, and photographs of him looking bloated and exhausted circulated widely, shocking many who still remembered the athletic figure of the 1980s.

The following year, Maradona's orbit briefly crossed with Italian club Perugia and the unlikely figure of Al-Saadi Gaddafi, son of Libyan revolutionary leader Muammar Gaddafi. Al-Saadi, who was more famous for his father's wealth than his talent, had managed, one way or another, to get himself a place in the Serie A side. His talent didn't ignite the Italian press and his team-mates weren't enamoured by the presence of his bodyguards around the training ground. Maradona, then drifting through the haze of semi-retirement, addiction struggles and celebrity appearances, accepted an offer to work with him as a sort of advisor and figurehead.

Some actual honour was bestowed upon Maradona in December 2003, when his former club, Argentinos Juniors, named their stadium after him. While most would argue that Diego's peak was around 1986, there is certainly a section of an older generation who swear blind that his actual peak was wearing the red shirt of *El Bicho*. That's open for debate, I guess.

By 2004, his health had deteriorated dramatically. Years of cocaine, alcohol, overeating and stress had pushed his body to the brink. In April of that year, he collapsed in Buenos Aires and was rushed to hospital with severe heart and lung problems. The news once again froze Argentina. Headlines screamed that he was dying, that this time there would be no return. Crowds gathered outside the hospital, chanting his name, praying, holding vigils. Television stations broadcast live updates 24 hours a day. The world watched as doctors spoke cautiously, as family members arrived in tears, as fans clung to hope.

Photographs from those days are seared into memory: Diego unconscious, intubated, machines keeping him alive. It was as if Argentina itself was in intensive care. The collective panic revealed just how deeply he was woven into the nation's identity. People said that if Diego died, Argentina would lose a piece of its soul. For weeks, it seemed possible. He hovered between life and death, his survival uncertain. Priests prayed for him, fans sang for him, newspapers prepared obituaries. But once again, as he had done so many times, Diego survived.

In 2004, Maradona came dangerously close to death. On 18 April, he was rushed to the Clínica Suizo-Argentina in Buenos Aires with a swollen heart, hypertension and respiratory collapse, was put into a medically induced coma and placed on a respirator. His condition remained critical in intensive care for several days – doctors described him as stable but heavily sedated, and the public watched with bated breath as the legend's body faltered. In early May he was discharged from the hospital and transferred to a rehab clinic for drug treatment, as relatives, media and legal authorities debated whether to commit him involuntarily for his addictions. His family actually considered petitioning a court to place him under psychiatric care, reflecting the desperate gravity of his state.

The 2004 crisis was more than a health scare – it was a reckoning. It forced Maradona back into treatment, drove further cracks in his relationships and briefly turned Argentina's greatest sporting icon into a tragic figure on life support. But even at his nadir, his public aura remained undiminished: fans gathered outside the clinic walls, banners were hung and phone lines to news outlets thundered with people seeking updates.

Public memory of those weeks in April 2004 remains vivid: Maradona lying in intensive care, sedated and on a ventilator, his life dependent on machines. The news bulletins were relentless, and Argentina reacted with a kind of national anxiety that spoke to his place in the country's identity. Commentators noted that if anything happened to him, it would feel as if the nation itself had lost a piece of its soul. For days his condition swung between hope and crisis, doctors issuing cautious updates and supporters gathering outside the clinic to wait for news. And yet, once again, Maradona pulled back from the brink. His survival became another chapter in the long, improbable saga of a man who had spent decades skirting the edge.

After his critical health crisis in April 2004, Maradona's family took legal and medical steps to control his care. Reports indicate the prospect of involuntary psychiatric or rehabilitation hospitalisation was under consideration. At the same time, his travel out of Argentina – specifically to Cuba, where he had previously lived and been treated – became entangled in familial and legal obstacles: relatives blocked his departure until legal processes opened the way for him to resume treatment abroad later that year.

Maradona's personal life was also entering a turbulent phase. He and Claudia Villafañe – his long-time partner and the mother of his daughters Dalma and Gianinna – finalised their divorce. The legal process revived old tensions and brought renewed scrutiny to his finances, property disputes and the responsibilities he carried toward his family. Argentine media often presented the breakdown of the marriage as part of a broader period of instability, linking it to the health scares, legal battles and erratic public appearances that increasingly defined his life.

On 22 June, 2005, he was officially presented as vice-president of Boca, charged with overseeing the first division squad and wielding influence over sporting decisions, with his contract to begin on 1 August. One of his first major moves in the position was recommending Alfio Basile as the new head coach – a decision that paid off as the team won multiple titles in the following seasons. Maradona's return to his beloved club's administration was not merely symbolic. He actively involved himself in transfers, coaching decisions and public relations, using both his name and football instincts to influence Boca's direction.

It was during this rebirth that Diego embarked on one of the strangest, most fascinating projects of his post-football life: his own television show, *La Noche del Diez*. Broadcast in 2005, it was a surreal spectacle: part variety show, part talk show, part confessional. Diego, dressed elegantly, slimmer than he had been in years, hosted celebrities from around the world. Guests included Roberto Gómez Bolaños, Pelé, Fidel Castro, Mike Tyson, Zinedine Zidane and countless Argentine stars. The show was chaotic, unpredictable, often bizarre, but always compelling – just like the host himself.

From the first episode, broadcast on Canal 13, it was clear this was not an ordinary show. The set was extravagant, lit like a stadium, the number 10 omnipresent in its design, with his former team-mate, and one of his former players when he was manager at Mandiyú, Sergio Goycochea as the show's co-host. The studio audience was packed with fans waving flags, chanting his name, turning the recording into a match-day atmosphere. When Diego walked onstage, dressed in suits or casual jackets, the crowd roared as though he had just scored against England again. He smiled, waved, kissed the air. He was at home, but it was a new kind of home. The ball was gone, but the stage remained.

An unforgettable moment came with Fidel Castro. Diego had long admired the Cuban leader, seeing in him not only politics but friendship. When he lived in Havana during his recovery from addiction, Fidel had welcomed him like a son. On the show, their conversation was both political and personal. They spoke of Cuba, of Latin America, of resistance to imperialism. Diego listened with respect, nodded and laughed. For Argentine television, it was extraordinary: a footballer turned host interviewing one of the most controversial figures of the 20th century. Critics accused him of propaganda. Admirers saw honesty, loyalty and conviction. Diego never pretended to be neutral. He was always, fiercely, himself.

La Noche del Diez was not only about famous guests. It was also about Diego's own life. The show frequently turned inward, revisiting his goals and his triumphs. Clips of Mexico 1986 played to roaring applause. Old team-mates appeared to embrace him. Fans sent messages of devotion. Diego wept on air, remembering his childhood, his struggles, his addictions. He laughed, he sang, he danced. The show was as much therapy for him as entertainment for the audience. It was Diego confronting his own myth, live, every week, in front of millions.

For Argentina, the show was a phenomenon. Ratings soared, streets emptied when it aired, families gathered around televisions as they once had for Boca-River matches. It was not polished, not professional, not perfect. But it was raw, authentic and magnetic. It was Diego. Every stutter, every misstep, every burst of laughter, every tear, every kiss – it was him, unfiltered.

Critics mocked his interviewing style, said he rambled and said he was ill-prepared. But the people loved him, because he was not pretending. He was not a trained host. He was Diego, talking as Diego always talked: with heart, with honesty, with passion.

Perhaps the most memorable highlight came when he welcomed Pelé, his old rival in the eternal debate of who was the greatest. The two embraced warmly, joked and sang together. For decades they had been compared, contrasted, sometimes at odds with one another. At the dawn of his career, a young Diego told reporters that he had no desire to follow in Pelé's footsteps – he only wanted to be himself. It was a bold statement, especially given the fierce sporting rivalry between Argentina and Brazil, and it captured his sense of destiny even then. Brazil had their global superstar, so Argentina were due theirs. They were different players, with completely different personalities. But both mesmerising in their own ways. When FIFA awarded the one-off Player of the Century for the greatest footballer of the 20th century in December 2000, it was jointly won by both Pelé and Maradona. Now, on Argentine television, they were smiling, heading the ball back and forth to one another.

English striker-turned-TV-presenter Gary Lineker visited Maradona at his Buenos Aires home for a BBC documentary at this time. The former Everton, Barcelona and Tottenham forward noted how Diego was back to looking his best, and how his left foot was still on first-name terms with the football, as evidenced by his high-profile cameo on the pitch at the charity fixture Soccer Aid. Lineker asked Diego if he was a director at Boca Juniors. Dressed in the club's famous blue and gold shirt and wearing a heavy necklace with a prominent cross at its centre, Diego grinned and announced he was an honorary president. The grin evaporated. He said he would be speaking with the president that week because a promised bonus had not been paid, then mimed clutching his own throat and warned he would seize the man here, like that, and make him explain himself publicly.

Maradona brought Lineker to La Bombonera for a Boca match against Quilmes. When the Englishman asked him what the atmosphere would be like, Diego told him it was unequalled anywhere else. The moment they arrived, the truth of that claim became obvious. Supporters surged toward him, cameras tracked his movements and the chants rolled down from every tier of the stadium. Fans called his name from all directions as he walked through the crowd, smiling broadly among his own people. Lineker – a major figure from Maradona's playing era and the top scorer at the 1986 World Cup – could only watch in awe as he witnessed the scale of devotion that enveloped Diego in his home country.

With the hierarchy at Boca, his time as vice-president would eventually conclude amid disputes with the Argentine Football Association (AFA), especially when Boca's coach, Alfio Basile, was selected to lead the national team – Maradona saw a conflict of interest and ultimately resigned in August 2006. He publicly said his role at Boca was 'a closed chapter' and warned incoming coach Ricardo La Volpe to respect the team's existing style. He also voiced displeasure with how AFA politics were handled around coaching moves.

After his resignation as vice-president of Boca Juniors, Maradona remained in the public eye by shifting his energies toward exhibition football and media spectacle. He toured Latin America with Showbol (indoor five-a-side) matches – scoring goals and drawing crowds in Honduras, El Salvador and Mexico – before returning to Argentina to host a marquee Argentina vs. Brazil Showbol evening at Luna Park, a large arena in downtown Buenos Aires close to Puerto Madero, in December. These appearances underscored that even out of formal power, his magnetism in the football world remained intact. Meanwhile, rumours about his health and substance use continued to swirl.

In late March 2007, Maradona was admitted to Sanatorio Güemes in Buenos Aires after suffering from a severe 'chemical, acute and toxic hepatitis,' largely attributed to years of excessive drinking. His condition was serious and he was kept under intensive care, while his medical team described him as 'stable' but still critical. On 11 April, Maradona was discharged from the hospital, only to be readmitted two days later when his abdominal pain worsened. In the following days, there were constant rumours about his health, including three false claims of his death within a month. But by 7 May, following weeks of treatment and hospitalisation,

Maradona was discharged from the psychiatric clinic. Just one day later, he appeared on Argentine television, declaring that he had quit alcohol and had not used drugs for two and a half years.

Diego rejoined the rhythm of public life: making appearances, speaking openly about recovery and spending time between Argentina and Cuba as part of ongoing treatment. He eventually appeared healthier, gave interviews and resumed attending matches. His recovery restored public sympathy, making him once again a visible national figure.

Maradona stayed close to the game. He was often present at Boca Juniors fixtures and high-profile events, and continued voicing strong opinions about Argentina's national team. Argentina's World Cup qualifying campaign had been shaky for months: after a strong start, the team fell into a run of inconsistency and draws – five matchdays without a win in qualifiers and friendlies had frustrated fans, media and the federation alike.

In October 2008 Argentina suffered a 1-0 defeat to Chile in Santiago. That loss badly undermined Basile's authority. Maradona was vocal about the result. Facing mounting criticism and what was described as 'anger from the public' over the Chile loss, Basile met with AFA president Julio Grondona and tendered his resignation, citing personal reasons. He later said he 'had pain in his heart'.

When Alfio Basile stepped down in October 2008, undone by a faltering qualifying campaign and a team adrift, a vacuum opened at the heart of Argentine football. The press, ever attuned to the scent of drama, immediately began to circulate names. Carlos Bianchi, the great architect of Boca's continental dominance, appeared the logical choice – the methodical winner with medals enough to silence any boardroom doubt. Sergio Batista, too, offered a steady hand, a sense of continuity from within. By any rational measure, the appointment should have followed the traditional logic of football governance: reward competence, lean on experience, minimise risk.

But Argentina has rarely been a land governed by logic. Beneath the formal process there flickered something more visceral – the lure of narrative, of salvation through charisma. For Grondona, Maradona was not simply a candidate; he was an idea. He had said for years that Diego was the man to lead Argentina from the dugout, the boy from Villa Fiorito elevated to national leader once more. In a country still haunted by its own footballing mythology, the appointment promised resurrection: the return of the chosen one to restore passion and pride. Whether it made sense was completely beside the point. In Argentina, and particularly under Grondona, symbolism had always mattered more than systems.

No other human on earth with a managerial CV like Maradona would get even close to such a prestigious job at an elite national team. But for many Argentinians, Diego Armando Maradona is unlike any other human.

CHAPTER SIX

The Divine Touchline

BY THE end of 2008, Argentina felt uneasy. The national team had lost its spark, the fans were restless and every debate ended with the same name – Diego. He was still the country's emotional shorthand for deliverance, the one figure who could turn despair into noise. Then, one overcast morning in Buenos Aires, whispers became headlines. Maradona was returning, not to play, not to inspire from afar, but to take charge. Outside the AFA building on Viamonte Street, journalists and cameramen crowded the pavement, waiting for proof that the miracle was real.

On 28 October 2008, under the soft spring sun of Buenos Aires, Diego Maradona met Julio Grondona to seal the agreement that would make him manager of Argentina. The announcement came later that day with the inevitable drama that followed him everywhere. At the AFA headquarters in the Ezeiza district, Maradona appeared before the press in a sharp suit and tie, flanked by Grondona and Carlos Bilardo – his former World Cup coach, now appointed general manager of the national side. Cameras jostled, journalists filled every inch of the room, and outside, fans gathered as though witnessing a coronation.

When he spoke, it was with the familiar mixture of humility and swagger that defined him. He called the job both an honour and a destiny, the final step in a life bound to the sky-blue and white. It was not simply employment; it was a sacred duty. He promised to give everything, to shape a team that would make the country proud, but beneath the confidence there was an unmistakable tremor of vulnerability. He asked for patience – time to grow into a role that no one could truly prepare for. The AFA confirmed his contract would run through the 2010 World Cup, assuming Argentina reached it, and immediately the media split into two camps: one hailing the romance of his return, the other warning that emotion was no substitute for experience.

The press conference was a spectacle. Maradona, slimmer than he had been for years, hair jet-black, eyes bright, spoke with a passion that made the room hum. The suit could barely contain him. As he looked out at the sea of cameras, he likened the moment to touching the sky – the same phrase he had used after lifting the World Cup in 1986. Then, he had carried a nation's dreams as its captain; now, he was inheriting them as its coach. The symbolism was irresistible. His 48th birthday was days away and he called the appointment a gift – a return, a reckoning, a revival. But even in celebration, unease lingered. Critics pointed to his limited managerial record, his health, his volatility.

Still, for Grondona and for millions of Argentines, the decision was not about logic. It was about faith. Argentina would once again rise or fall with Diego.

On 19 November, a few weeks after the announcement, Maradona finally took charge, for a friendly against Scotland at Hampden Park, Glasgow – the very stadium at which he had scored his first international goal back in 1979. This time, the *Albiceleste* (a nickname for the Argentina team, meaning literally 'white and sky blue') secured a 1–0 victory, with Maxi Rodríguez scoring the decisive goal. It was a cautious, measured start rather than a flourish, but for Maradona it was a moment of vindication – stepping into the dugout not as the prodigal son returning, but as a national coach under the glaring lights.

His next match in charge was 84 days later, when the *Albiceleste* travelled to Marseille to take on France at the Stade Vélodrome in another friendly. In front of 60,000, Maradona's men managed to defeat Raymond Domenech's French side 2-0, with goals from Jonas Gutiérrez and a young man named Lionel Messi.

The press made a big deal over which Argentinian would be the 'next Maradona'. The names bandied about were serious ones in the sport – Tevez, Riquelme, Saviola, Aimar, Ariel Ortega. But it was Messi who Diego appointed as his 'successor' in Argentinian football. Messi was globally known for being unique, skilful and utterly brilliant and drew comparisons with Diego even very early on in his career. Messi's close control of the ball, speed, skill and flair were identical to Maradona's. The young man from Rosario was above most of the names ever mentioned in the same sentence as Diego Maradona. Now the coach of the national team had a truly unique talent at his disposal. They were two of the greatest to ever play the game, on the same side – one as manager, one as player.

Having made his debut three years prior, a section of Argentina fans didn't take to the Barcelona star as quickly as they had done to Diego when the latter started playing in the national side. Messi had been plucked from Newell's Old Boys underage groups at the age of 13 and signed for Barça's youth academy, La Masia, with the promise that the Catalans would pay for his relatively expensive growth hormone therapy to help with his small stature. He never played club football in Argentina professionally. So there was a small section who saw Messi as essentially a product of foreign investment, whereas if you said to a Barcelona supporter that Messi was one of their own, they'd laugh at you. Despite being adored on the Spanish coast, it was a weird limbo scenario. On the other side of the south Atlantic there was no question that he was admired, but also judged harshly when the team failed. But it didn't matter – Messi was undeniably and proudly Argentine, with *mate*, the national drink of Argentina, almost always in his hand, his strong Argentinian accent and phrases spoken to the Spanish press. Maradona knew that the young lad was immensely proud of where he was from. He knew he was a phenomenal talent. Having watched him win a gold medal for Argentina at the

2008 Olympic Games in Beijing, Diego knew this kid would always give 100 per cent.

At 48 years old, Maradona had become a grandfather for the first time, when his younger daughter, Gianinna gave birth to Benjamín Agüero Maradona – the son of Gianinna and Sergio 'Kun' Agüero, a rising star at Atlético Madrid. Argentine newspapers such as *Clarín* and *Olé* splashed the story across their front pages, calling him '*el abuelo más famoso del mundo*' – 'the most famous grandfather in the world'. Beaming as he left the hospital, Diego told reporters, '*Estoy muy feliz. Es un maradonita más.*' – 'I'm very happy. He's another little Maradona.'

Diego Maradona's debut competitive fixture took place on 28 March 2009. The World Cup qualifier was played at the Estadio Monumental, where Argentina comfortably defeated Venezuela 4–0. Goals from Lionel Messi, Carlos Tevez, Maxi Rodríguez and Sergio Agüero sealed a commanding victory, marking a confident opening to Maradona's tenure in matches that counted.

A few days later, the *Albiceleste* travelled to La Paz to face Bolivia, where the match, played at a staggering 3,600m above sea level, ended in a shocking 6–1 defeat for Argentina, their worst result in decades. Unacclimatised to the conditions, the players struggled and Maradona stood helpless on the sideline, watching his team collapse. The press tore him apart. Critics said he was a cheerleader, not a coach. Opponents mocked him. International media declared Maradona's managerial career over already.

Diego, defiant as always, refused to bow. He insisted the altitude was to blame. However, when FIFA had imposed a temporary ban on playing at altitudes of 2,500m and above just three years prior, Maradona had been incredibly vocal against the decision. To protest he had flown to Bolivia and played in an exhibition match at Estadio Hernando Siles in La Paz, highlighting to football's governing body that football could still be played competitively at high altitudes. Maradona's team secured a 7–4 victory that day over a Bolivian team led by President Evo Morales.

FIFA repealed the decision in May 2008. Now, Maradona was awkwardly using it as an excuse. He insisted his team would recover regardless, and fight on.

The months that followed were a rollercoaster. Argentina lurched between narrow wins and painful defeats, each match a national drama. The players themselves seemed unsettled, caught between reverence for Diego and frustration at the lack of clarity. Riquelme, one of Argentina's most gifted playmakers, clashed with him and retired from the national team, declaring he could not play under Maradona's style. It was a blow, but Diego shrugged it off, saying he wanted players who gave everything, who bled for the shirt.

And always, in the background, the figure of Messi loomed. Diego embraced him constantly, praised him and protected him. But Messi struggled to replicate his Barcelona brilliance in the *Albiceleste* shirt. The comparisons to Maradona were relentless and the fact that Maradona himself was on the bench only intensified them. Fans begged for Messi to become the new Diego, but Messi was Messi: quiet, introverted, methodical. Diego was volcanic, explosive, instinctive. The tension between their identities defined this period, even as they smiled for cameras together.

The pressure mounted further in September when Argentina hosted Brazil in Rosario, only to be beaten 3–1 in front of their own supporters. That result left Maradona's side in danger of missing out on automatic qualification for the 2010 World Cup, and things worsened when they lost 1–0 to Paraguay in Asunción a few days later, with Nelson Valdez scoring the decisive goal. However, they then rallied, edging out Peru 2–1 in Buenos Aires, thanks to a dramatic late goal from Martín Palermo in torrential rain, a moment that became symbolic of Argentina's survival instincts.

Argentina's qualification still hung by a thread. The nation was in agony. To imagine a World Cup without Argentina was unthinkable. To imagine Maradona failing in this role was unbearable. The pressure was immense, the criticism savage, the atmosphere hysterical. And yet, in typical Diego fashion, when the abyss loomed, he found a way to pull Argentina back. In the final qualifying match in October, Argentina defeated Uruguay in Montevideo to secure their place in South Africa. Diego ran across the pitch in celebration, arms outstretched, shouting, embracing his players. He had done it. Against all odds, against all critics, Argentina were going to the World Cup.

And then, in the post-match press conference, he delivered the phrase that would define the era: '*Que la chupen. Que la sigan chupando.*' 'Let them suck it. Let them keep sucking.' It was his response to the journalists who had criticised him, his defiant victory cry: crude, vulgar, quintessentially Diego. The room gasped, the world reported it with astonishment, the AFA fined him. But the people, the fans, roared with laughter and love. That was Diego. He spoke as they spoke, without filter, without fear, with passion. He had taken Argentina to the World Cup, and he had done it his way.

Maradona's tactics and decisions had been under the spotlight for some time. He had sought to shake up the national setup early, experimenting with squad selections, tactics and player roles in the months before the tournament. He called up an unusually large pool of players, including many domestically based ones, in part to test depth and loyalty. He tried out different formations in training (e.g. 4-3-3), but often reverted to a 4-4-2 setup because, as he later admitted, in trial sessions the more attacking scheme 'did not penetrate the defence'. Meanwhile, Maradona also reintroduced veteran names: for example, Martín Palermo – absent from the national team for a decade and by now an icon at Boca Juniors – was recalled and subsequently scored that decisive last-minute goal in qualifying.

Diego's preparations also involved physical and logistical groundwork in South Africa. In early 2010, he visited the country and inspected Argentina's proposed base at the University of Pretoria's High Performance

Centre, expressing satisfaction with security, facilities and overall conditions. He publicly dismissed concerns about safety, saying his players should focus solely on football when the tournament arrived. Such efforts reflect that Maradona, despite his unpredictability, was conscious of needing to stabilise the environment around the team ahead of its appearance on the global stage.

Leading up to the trip to the World Cup, Argentina played a series of friendly matches designed to test the squad and sharpen fitness after a turbulent qualification campaign. A month after the game in Montevideo, the squad travelled to Madrid to face Spain at Atlético's now-demolished Calderón stadium, on the banks of the Manzanares river. In front of a full house, they succumbed to a 2–1 defeat.

By January, a largely domestic-based team beat Costa Rica 3–2, a game that gave Maradona the chance to experiment with players outside the European spotlight. Just a couple of weeks later, on 10 February, Argentina edged Jamaica 2–1, again leaning on fringe players and domestic talent as Maradona weighed his options.

More serious preparation began in early March, when Argentina travelled to Munich to face Germany. On 3 March 2010, they produced one of their most encouraging displays under Maradona, winning 1–0 thanks to a Gonzalo Higuaín goal. The performance was disciplined, with Argentina showing defensive solidity and tactical organisation, qualities often absent during qualifying. This victory over a top European side raised confidence that Maradona's team might yet find the right balance before the World Cup.

As the tournament drew closer, Diego fine-tuned his squad with confidence-boosting wins. On 5 May 2010, Argentina defeated Haiti 4–0, a match aimed more at boosting morale than providing a difficult opponent. Their final send-off fixture came on 24 May, when they beat Canada 5–0 in Buenos Aires, with Lionel Messi, Carlos Tevez and others showcasing attacking flair in front of an adoring home crowd. The emphatic victory set a celebratory tone as the squad departed for South Africa, where expectations were high despite lingering doubts about Maradona's tactical acumen.

The mood in Argentina heading into the 2010 World Cup was a complex mix of excitement, relief and deep anxiety. On one hand, the team boasted an extraordinary pool of attacking talent – Messi, Tevez, Higuaín, Diego Milito, Agüero – a forward line many considered the envy of world football. Many journalists, however, described Argentina as unpredictable: capable of brilliance, but just as likely to implode.

CHAPTER SEVEN

A Cathedral of Plastic Horns

THE COUNTRY held its breath as the list dropped. Every newsroom, every café, every taxi radio waited for the names – the 23 men who would carry Argentina's flag to South Africa under Diego's command. Outside the AFA building, reporters smoked nervously in the autumn sun; inside, Maradona sat before a wall of microphones, fingers drumming the table, eyes glittering with mischief. He knew what the announcement meant. It wasn't just a squad list – it was a declaration of faith.

When Maradona announced his squad for the tournament, attention quickly turned to those missing: Javier Zanetti and Esteban Cambiasso, two of Argentina's most seasoned figures. Both had just completed extraordinary campaigns with Inter Milan, lifting a historic treble under José Mourinho. Yet Maradona chose to omit them, insisting he wanted players who had endured the long grind of qualification rather than late arrivals. *Clarín* labelled the omissions baffling, questioning how two players in such form could be ignored. Maradona brushed off the criticism, saying his group reminded him of 1986 – a squad, he believed, made up entirely of warriors.

The World Cup of 2010 was the first to be held on African soil, and from the moment South Africa was awarded the tournament, it was clear that this would be a World Cup unlike any other. For Argentina, it was another chance to redeem themselves after years of inconsistency, and for one Diego Armando Maradona, it was a stage made for theatre. By the time the Argentina squad landed in South Africa, the chaos of the media focussed on their manager. He had survived the humiliations, the defeats, the insults, and had dragged his team to the tournament through sheer willpower and defiance. Now, with the world's eyes on him, he was determined not just to compete but to dominate the narrative, to remind everyone that wherever Diego stood, football became a myth.

From the very beginning, he was the star of the show. Coaches are usually secondary figures at World Cups, their names known but their faces confined to technical areas, their gestures noticed only by obsessives. Maradona shattered that convention. Cameras sought him constantly, panning to his face after every goal, lingering on his celebrations, capturing his embraces with players, his leaps, his shouts, his wild charisma. On the sidelines he was as magnetic as he had once been on the pitch. He wore sharp suits, heavy watches, his hair slightly longer, his beard streaked with grey. He paced like a caged animal, gesticulated wildly, shouted instructions that often seemed more emotional than tactical. The world was transfixed. Here was Maradona, the genius of 1986, now the father figure of Argentina in 2010.

The build-up to Argentina's opener against Nigeria was drenched in anticipation and doubt. Maradona, now leading his country from the dugout, carried the weight of a turbulent qualifying campaign in which Argentina had stumbled, losing heavily in La Paz and scraping into the tournament in the final rounds. Critics questioned his tactics and even his temperament. Lionel Messi, now the reigning FIFA World Player of the Year, was expected to finally blossom in a World Cup, carrying the dreams of a nation still longing for a successor to their 1986 triumph. Maradona, meanwhile, framed the moment with characteristic bravado, telling reporters that Argentina were ready 'to fight for the cup with our hearts'. The stage was set not only for a football match, but for the beginning of a story that would test whether the most mercurial player in Argentina's history could succeed as its coach.

Ellis Park Stadium in Johannesburg was the setting for the opening match for the *Albiceleste*. The stadium, packed with vuvuzelas that produced a constant drone like a swarm of bees, buzzed with anticipation. Diego walked on to the pitch in his grey suit, hugged his players, kissed Messi, waved to the stands. The cameras followed his every move. When the anthem played, he sang with gusto, his eyes moist, his fists clenched. And then the game began, and Argentina looked alive.

An early headed goal by Gabriel Heinze in the sixth minute was enough for Diego's men to secure the victory. Heinze met a corner from Juan Sebastián Verón with a diving header that flew into the top corner. Despite Argentina's attacking firepower – Messi, Gonzalo Higuaín, Carlos Tevez, and Ángel Di María all started – the team failed to add to the scoreline, thanks largely to a heroic performance from Nigeria's goalkeeper Vincent Enyeama, who made several crucial saves, especially from Messi.

After the match, Maradona praised his team's intensity but was openly frustrated by their wastefulness in front of goal. He lamented that Argentina's finishing lacked the ruthlessness required at this level, saying he had warned his players that in football, mercy is a luxury no team can afford. Missed chances, he reminded them, always come back with interest – the game punishes those who hesitate, no matter how beautifully they play in between.

Verón picked up a calf injury in the Nigeria match, and was ruled out of the next game. Maradona announced that they would rest him rather than risk worsening the injury, and would replace him with Maxi Rodríguez for the South Korea match which was due to take place in five days' time. In the run-up to the second group match, news outlets noted that Argentina's training sessions were under close scrutiny: Maradona was contemplating 'shoring up his defence' given they had played more offensively against Nigeria.

At a packed press conference before the match against South Korea, Maradona turned the spotlight away from tactics and on to old rivals. Reports had surfaced that Pelé had mocked his appointment, suggesting he had only taken the Argentina job for the money. Diego's response was swift and cutting, dismissing the Brazilian with characteristic bite and reminding everyone that their feud, decades long, was far from over. He also took aim toward Michel Platini, the UEFA president and another of football's grand old figures, describing their relationship as cold and distant – polite on the surface, but never ever warm. Beneath his words ran the familiar undercurrent of resentment toward European football's establishment, which he often accused of condescension toward South Americans. It was pure Maradona: defiant, theatrical, unwilling to let anyone else write his story.

Argentina produced their most emphatic performance of the group stage on 17 June, dismantling South Korea 4–1 at Soccer City in Johannesburg. The first breakthrough came on 16 minutes when Messi's free-kick delivery deflected off Martín Demichelis and wrong-footed Park Chu-Young, going down as an own goal. Soon after, a well-worked corner routine saw Nicolás Burdisso flick the ball on for Higuaín to head home Argentina's second. Just before half-time, however, Demichelis was punished for a lapse, dispossessed by Lee Chung-Yong who calmly chipped Sergio Romero to give South Korea a lifeline.

In the second half, Maradona's team reasserted control and Higuaín stole the headlines. Messi, orchestrating from deep, twice broke South Korea's lines

– first hitting the post before Higuaín tapped in the rebound, then sliding a pass to Sergio Agüero, whose cross found Higuaín for a simple header. The hat-trick made Higuaín the first Argentine to score three in a World Cup match since Gabriel Batistuta in 1998. The result all but guaranteed Argentina's passage to the knockout stage and temporarily silenced doubts over Maradona's tactical approach, with Messi's freedom and Argentina's set-piece sharpness hailed as decisive.

After the match, Maradona entered the mixed zone to a plethora of microphones waiting for him, with a swagger undone only by fatigue. He was buoyant, by his own telling, but the edge was there – the same edge that had shaped his playing years, now channelled through the megaphone of management. He lauded his team's 'greatness', especially Higuaín's finishing, calling the hat-trick 'a gift from God'. Yet even in victory, Maradona could not resist returning to the themes he'd ranted about before: the ball, the critics, the doubters. In five days' time they would have their third and final group match.

The air in Polokwane crackled with expectation – Argentina had two wins, but Maradona knew the final group game was no mere formality. Greece, clinging to slivers of hope, had to fight, and would do so with a defensive ambition that mirrored their German coach Otto Rehhagel's reputation. Commentators noted that Maradona, having already rotated and nursed players through the first two matches, might again tinker: who to rest, who to push forward, how much freedom to give

Messi now that the burden had lessened. In whispered corridors of the team hotel and press rooms, speculation swirled: would a cautious line-up betray fear or smart resource management?

The stage was set. Argentina were already through, yet the world watched to see how Maradona would juggle pragmatism and spectacle. He rotated heavily, making seven changes, resting Messi, Tevez, Higuaín and Mascherano from the start. After kick-off, the first hour felt more like probing than poetry for Argentina.

Then the deadlock broke. On 77 minutes, Demichelis thumped home after a corner fell kindly in the box. Just 12 minutes later, substitute Martín Palermo, at 36 years old and improbably present at his first World Cup, scored Argentina's second, pouncing on a rebound after Messi's shot was parried . That goal was greeted with delight not just in Argentina but across the footballing world. Palermo had been the hero of countless Boca nights, the man of impossible stories, now finally etched into the World Cup chronicle. Maradona, who had hand-picked him for the squad, celebrated like a proud father. Argentina's 2–0 win meant they topped the group with maximum points, and though questions remained about the defence and shape, the mood was buoyant. It was less about the performance, more about destiny – Argentina rolling forward with Maradona orchestrating both theatre and football.

After cruising through the group stage undefeated, Argentina now faced a familiar foe in Mexico. In the days before kick-off, Maradona attempted to balance respect and swagger. He declared that Mexico had 'players who concern us', but insisted Argentina would demand their own due – that the 'history' of the *Albiceleste* shouldn't be taken lightly. Meanwhile, Mexican coach Javier Aguirre leaned into the 'underdog' role, telling the media that no one was tipping Mexico and that they intended to defy expectations.

It was back to Johannesburg for Diego's men and the affair was as dramatic as it was controversial. It finished 3–1 to Argentina, sending Maradona's side into the quarter-finals, but the scoreline was shaped as much by refereeing chaos as by Argentina's superiority.

The opening goal arrived in the 26th minute: Messi chipped a delicate ball forward that found Tevez, who was clearly offside. The flag should have gone up but the Italian referee, Roberto Rosetti, allowed play to continue and Tevez headed home. Mexican players surrounded the officials in fury, and even on the giant stadium screens the replay showed the error. The protests, however, were waved away. Argentina doubled their lead minutes later when Ricardo Osorio, under pressure, misplaced a back pass straight into Higuaín's path. The striker rounded the keeper and finished calmly for his fourth goal of the tournament.

In the second half, Tevez struck again, this time with a thunderous shot from outside the area that flew into the top corner – no controversy, just brilliance. Mexico's consolation came through Javier 'Chicharito' Hernández, who spun Demichelis in the box and smashed past Sergio Romero to make it 3–1. Despite that goal, Argentina always looked in control, their attacking quartet – Messi, Tevez, Higuaín, Di María – fluid and menacing. Yet the shadow of that first offside goal lingered, with Mexican players and fans feeling robbed. Maradona, animated on the touchline, celebrated wildly, pointing to the heavens after each goal, already casting Argentina's campaign as destiny-driven.

The victory set up a mouth-watering quarter-final against Germany. But more than that, it reinforced the dual nature of Maradona's Argentina: dazzling, chaotic, blessed and blemished, their fate a mixture of genius and controversy. Onwards to Cape Town for a fixture against a team Argentina, and Maradona especially, knew oh so well.

The game began with the crack of inevitability: Thomas Müller, barely three minutes in, rose to meet a Bastian Schweinsteiger free kick and planted a header past Romero. From then on, Germany moved through Argentina as if through warm air, fluid in possession, sharp on transitions, while Argentina looked stranded, disordered, overexposed. Germany's press was surgical; Argentina's structure dissolved under pressure.

In the second half, the fault lines deepened. Striker Miroslav Klose tapped in a second goal after a precise break, Arne Friedrich sprinted and finished a third, and Klose volleyed a fourth in the 89th minute, turning what might've been a close exit into a rout. The Argentine players were shadows of themselves: Messi compressed by defenders, Higuaín starved of service, the midfield unable to recover balance. In the wake, Tevez would say the hurt lay in *not* playing as a team and trying to rely on individual flashes of brilliance.

Maradona, whose swagger and prophecy had carried the team so far, watched helplessly as his dream collapsed in waves of German precision. He raged, he gestured, he tried to inspire, but there was no miracle. The cameras showed him biting his lip, shaking his head, clapping his players, but his eyes betrayed his despair. For a man who had carried Argentina to glory as a player, to watch them collapse as a coach was agony. When the final whistle blew, he walked on to the pitch, hugged his players, kissed Messi and whispered to them. He did not blame them. He carried the pain himself. The television cameras in the tunnel captured Maradona being embraced by his daughter, Dalma, while Germany manager Joachim Löw stood in the background awkwardly so he could shake Diego's hand. In the post-match silence, it felt less like elimination and more like unravelling.

The Argentine press responded with something between grief and rage. The tone was largely unforgiving: in the days that followed, newspapers described the elimination as a 'worst end' to their World Cup hopes, lamented the team's lack of answers and questioned Maradona's future at the helm. At home and abroad, the consensus was that Maradona had no idea what he was doing. It was easy to blame Diego for everything wrong with Argentina, yet in truth he fared no worse than his predecessors at the World Cup.

'Not since 1990 has Argentina made it past the quarter-finals,' he reminded critics. 'Nobody is talking about that.' Only César Menotti and Carlos Bilardo have ever lifted the World Cup as Argentina managers. The last time the *Albiceleste* reached a final was with Bilardo at the helm and Maradona as captain, when they fell to Germany at Italia '90.

In 1998, Daniel Passarella's team were undone by a single flash of genius from Dennis Bergkamp. Then came 2002: Argentina arrived in Japan and South Korea on the back of a breathtaking qualifying campaign, but with the nation itself in economic freefall, Marcelo Bielsa's side crashed out in the group stage. Germany 2006 is remembered less for Argentina's talent than for José Pekerman's fateful decision to withdraw Juan Román Riquelme, a change that allowed the hosts to seize control of the quarter-final and knock the *Albiceleste* out.

Reflecting on this cycle of frustration, Maradona argued it was no accident: 'It's because things aren't being done properly up above, and nothing is being done to change it,' he said, accusing those in charge of caring more for 'their bank balance than for Argentinian football'.

After Argentina's exit, Maradona was forced to confront not just sporting failure, but internal politics. He publicly admitted he was reconsidering his future, saying, 'I may leave tomorrow.' In the week that followed, the AFA floated a new four-year deal, suggesting they might keep him on through to the

2014 World Cup. But behind that public overture lay friction: AFA president Julio Grondona and other board members insisted Maradona change his backroom staff. Maradona resisted – he saw loyalty to his complete inner circle as a point of pride and personal code.

Asking him to change his backroom staff may appear to be a reasonable request from the AFA. But the real motivation was not to improve the quality of advice Maradona received. Carlos Bilardo regularly clashed with Maradona's two right-hand men, Alejandro Mancuso and Héctor Enrique, and amid the post-World Cup mess, Bilardo would be staying on at the AFA. By requesting that Maradona sack seven of his team, Grondona was effectively sacking Maradona because he knew he would not stay without them.

Ironically, the dynamic was captured best by Miguel Ángel Lemme – one of the few assistants Maradona himself had pushed out months earlier – who described the relationship between Bilardo and Maradona as 'like Tom and Jerry'. His reign as coach often drifted toward caricature, edging into farce, with the two men locked in a duel that frequently felt less like collaboration than a cartoon stalemate.

But the inevitable was going to happen. Maradona met Grondona in Buenos Aires in a last attempt to secure his future, but Maradona made his conditions clear: he would only continue if his entire backroom staff remained intact.

When Grondona relayed the outcome of those talks to the board, the verdict was ruthless. The AFA released a statement that read: 'The president of the Argentinian Football Association, Mr Julio Grondona, informed the executive committee of his conversation with Mr Diego Maradona, outlining the key points that emerged from the meeting. The executive committee unanimously resolved not to renew the contract with Mr Diego Maradona as coach of the Argentina national football team.'

And so it ended for Maradona at the helm of Argentina. Inevitable? Maybe. But had it been good to watch him on the touchline for his beloved country? It had been mesmerising. He had prowled the technical area with the same restless energy he once showed on the pitch, gesturing wildly, barking instructions, embracing his players as if they were brothers. For a while, it felt like Argentina were being led not by a manager but by a living myth, a man whose passion and volatility mirrored the nation itself. His tenure may have been chaotic, his tactics erratic, but his presence was theatre – raw, unfiltered, impossible to ignore. Diego Maradona's greatest victory, even in failure, even in humiliation, was that he remained loved, adored, eternal. The World Cup of 2010 was not his glory. But it was his theatre, his opera, his tragedy. And like all great tragedies, it left him larger than life, unforgettable, immortal.

CHAPTER EIGHT

Silence After the Songs

THE INK on his dismissal was barely dry when the whispers began again. Maradona, restless as ever, refused to fade quietly. He wanted another bench, another stage – anywhere that would still have him. Reporters caught the scent first: murmurs from London, talk of meetings, of phone calls, of a Premier League adventure. The idea alone was deliciously improbable – the man who broke English hearts in '86, stalking the touchlines of Birmingham.

Mere weeks after being let go from the national team job, Maradona fancied himself a gig in the Premier League in England. His European representative, Walter Soriano, claimed at the time that the 49-year-old was in discussions with several clubs, including one in England, and even suggested Maradona would have been open to an approach from Aston Villa.

'If the owner Randy Lerner wants to make him a serious offer, I am sure he would get a very positive response,' Soriano said, stressing that Maradona was carefully considering his options. Although his reputation in England remained scarred by the infamous 'Hand of God' goal of 1986, the words 'genius' and 'cheat' are so often put together by the British media when mentioning Maradona, the rumours created a stir – though Villa swiftly dismissed the possibility of appointing him.

'It is the saddest birthday of my life,' Maradona confessed on his 50th birthday, his voice heavy with bitterness. Three months had passed since the AFA declined to renew his contract as national coach. The wound of that refusal was deep: he felt cast adrift from the team he had poured himself into, removed from the institution he loved, left to mourn what might have been. 'The best gift would have been continuing with the national team,' he said. 'When we were knocked out of the World Cup, I began my mourning period.'

That birthday, meant to mark half a century of existence, of triumph and struggle, instead became a moment of resignation. His legacy as a player was untouchable; his ambitions as a coach, fragile. The public tone of anguish masked something more volatile: indignation. He felt betrayed not merely by decision-makers, but by fate itself.

The cracks in his managerial ambitions deepened when Boca Juniors, the club most intimately bound to Maradona's myth, turned toward appointing Julio César Falcioni as their coach. To Diego, it was more than a snub: it was a betrayal by the club that had claimed him, raised him, made him legend. He publicly mocked Falcioni's credentials, sneering that he was 'just a goalkeeper', and lambasted Boca's president, Jorge Amor Ameal, for failing to see his own debt to Diego. 'They turn their back on someone who was made by them,' he fumed. 'One day I will sit on Boca's bench.'

The irony was brutal: at this stage in his life, Maradona was not a candidate judged purely on tactical acumen or a record of wins and losses. To hire Maradona was to hire spectacle, to grasp a global name that guaranteed headlines, that conferred instant legitimacy. In an era where elite football was evolving – Guardiola's Barcelona redefining positional play; German teams reviving pressing; Spanish tiki-taka creating new paradigms – Maradona offered something no coach in a suit could: Diego. The narrative, the lure, the existential weight of his name.

Yet that very weight also worked against him. Clubs and federations fretted over his instability, his health, his unpredictability, his celebrity. To embrace him implied that one would also sign up for scandal, spectacle, emotional turbulence. The football world had perhaps grown too professional, too risk-averse, to let a myth manage.

Maradona's refusal to fire his staff when the AFA demanded it was not merely loyalty; it was a moral stand. To abandon his confidants would have meant compromising his identity. To him, the coaches, physiotherapists, psychologists and aides were part of a 'family' – intrinsic to how he worked, how he trusted. To strip them was to hollow the structure around him. The association's insistence wounded both his ego and his sense of coherence. Not surprisingly, he later threatened legal action, accusing AFA president Julio Grondona of spreading damaging rumours about his personal life in order to justify the dismissal.

There is a tragic symmetry in this conflict: Maradona, once the player who bent the laws of physics on a pitch, now found himself constrained by institutional law – by contracts, by politics, by expectations. The same defiant spirit that dribbled past defenders now tussled with boardrooms.

Meanwhile, Boca Juniors' appointment of Falcioni – a man of steel-rimmed pragmatism rather than expressive flair – revealed more than a simple managerial choice. It exposed the widening gap between football's living myth and the corporate modernity that had come to define the club. Falcioni, who had won admiration for guiding modest Banfield to a league title, was respected but not adored. He was a coach who valued order over improvisation, rigidity over romance. To Boca's hierarchy, still reeling from years of inconsistency, he represented safety, control and quiet authority. But to Diego Maradona, watching from the sidelines, the decision cut like betrayal.

In the months that followed, his fury spilled across microphones and television screens. Maradona did not merely criticise; he waged a campaign of emotional resistance. 'I would die to be Boca's coach,' he declared, his voice trembling between pride and desperation. The statement was not rhetorical – it was confessional. Coaching Boca would have been more than a job; it would have been a form of redemption, a reunion with the only temple that had never fully abandoned him.

When that door closed, it reopened every old wound. He accused club president Ameal of betrayal, claiming he had been promised consideration only to be 'erased' from contention. To reporters, he said Boca had 'turned its back on its own blood'.

Behind these public eruptions, there was desperation. Diego's identity after his playing days was fractured. The field, where he had been alive, was gone. His coaching stints never matched his goals as a player. The financial, personal and health pressures mounted. He hoped to return to the national team or take on club work abroad. But the doors were closing.

The dynamic is more than personal bitterness; it is a myth in collision with modern governance. Maradona had moved from being a force in the pitch's flow to an agent in the institutional ebb. He rebelled against contractual limits, felt the coldness of club boards, chafed under administrative authority. The stadiums still sang his name – but boardrooms no longer yielded. His aspiration to manage Boca was not only ambition, but a desire for reconciliation: to bind his legend to a place, to anchor himself in a locale that once embraced him.

In May 2011, Maradona flew to Chechnya with a handful of big-name former stars to play in an exhibition match that bordered on the surreal. Grozny's new stadium, freshly built and gleaming under a tense, theatrical sky, filled to capacity as tens of thousands of Chechens arrived, eager to witness a spectacle unlike anything they had seen. On one side stood the local team, led on the field by Chechen leader, Ramzan

Kadyrov, dressed in full kit and eager to demonstrate both political strength and sporting glamour. On the other, a star-studded 'world team' featuring Robbie Fowler, Franco Baresi, Luis Figo and, at its magnetic centre, Diego Armando Maradona. The match was less about football than symbolism – reconciliation, propaganda, nostalgia – but Diego played it earnestly, smiling for cameras, enjoying the adoration.

Then, almost from nowhere, came an unexpected call: an offer from Dubai.

CHAPTER NINE

The Prophet in the Desert

THE DOORS of the plane opened to heat that seemed to breathe. It wasn't weather so much as a presence – a heavy, invisible animal that wrapped itself around his chest as he stepped on to the tarmac. The desert air shimmered, bending the horizon. For a moment, Diego lifted his hand to shield his eyes and it looked like the old salute to the crowd, the same gesture he had made in Naples, in Buenos Aires, in Mexico City. Only now there were no terraces, no chants – just a line of men in white robes and gold sunglasses, waiting politely behind a rope barrier.

He smiled anyway. He always smiled when he arrived. Cameras clicked. Someone shouted '*Maradona! Bienvenido a Dubái*!' in an accent he'd never heard before. It didn't matter. The syllables of his name carried across every language. He patted his chest, pointed to the sky, and whispered, '*Gracias, Dios.*'

From the airport, the motorcade rolled through a city that felt half-real, half-mirage. Towers shaped like flames and sails, fountains leaping out of marble plazas, a skyline growing faster than belief. Billboards already bore his face – the halo of curls, the stubborn eyes. Beneath them, workers in yellow vests stared up as if they'd seen a saint.

He had come to Dubai to take up a contract with Al Wasl – a two-year deal, worth $5 million, and accommodation in a villa with private security. At his first press conference, Maradona sat behind a table draped with gold cloth, the Al Wasl club crest embroidered like a crown. Reporters from across the Gulf jostled for position. When it was his turn to speak, he leaned toward the microphone and smiled that old magician's smile. 'I'm here,' he said, 'because football is the same language everywhere – it speaks to the heart, not the wallet.'

The translators struggled to keep up. Flashbulbs burst. And for a moment – just a moment – the old electricity returned. The man who had defied empires was back on a stage, even if this one was air-conditioned.

For Diego, Dubai was unlike anything he had known. He had lived in Naples, in Buenos Aires, in Havana, in Barcelona. Dubai was like another world: skyscrapers like monuments to excess, malls the size of towns, artificial islands carved into the sea. It was a city built on enormous oil wealth and enormous ambition, a playground for the global elite.

In interviews during his time there, Diego expressed fascination with Dubai's grandeur, but also a kind of alienation. He spoke warmly of the people, of their hospitality, but occasionally bristled at the lack of passion around the matches. In Argentina, football was life and death. In Dubai, it was rarely a spectacle. Diego longed for the madness of La Bombonera, but here he found families sitting politely, sipping drinks in air-conditioned stadiums.

From day one, expectations were high: Maradona brought in reinforcements from South America and Europe, threw himself into the role with theatrical flair and created a buzz around the club rarely seen in the UAE. He had inherited a squad blending local Emirati talents and foreign imports. Key names included Juan Manuel Olivera, Mariano Donda and Richard Porta. The Dubai press briefly buzzed. Ticket sales briefly rose. Al Wasl shirts with Diego's face printed on them appeared in shops. It was a new era.

There were nights of joy. A 3–0 win against Al Jazira in the Etisalat Cup showed what Diego wanted: fast transitions, quick interplay, joy in attack. There were also nights of humiliation: a 5–0 defeat to Dubai CSC, where the defence collapsed entirely. The press, both local and international, began to question him. Was Maradona really coaching, or simply cheerleading? He was often seen pacing the touchline furiously, gesticulating, shouting instructions. But tactical adjustments were rare. Substitutions were impulsive, sometimes baffling.

In February 2012, during a league match against Al Shabab, tensions flared and after the game Maradona was involved in a confrontation with opposition fans. Shouting escalated, objects were thrown and Diego had to be restrained by security. The images went viral: Maradona, at 51 years old, still fighting, still furious, still incapable of calm. He later defended himself, saying he was protecting his players from insults. But the club was embarrassed. Just the previous month, Diego had been on a shortlist to manage the UAE national team. Not likely now.

Maradona's ambitions for Al Wasl were never small. He wanted the club to roar, not whisper – to be a name recognised beyond the Gulf, a side that could make even European audiences glance eastward. He urged the board to think big, to use their wealth not for convenience but for spectacle. Big names, global attention, packed stands: that was his vision. When rumours began to swirl about a move for Didier Drogba, it seemed almost too audacious to be true. The Ivorian was still a force in world football, a symbol of power and prestige. The Emirati media treated the story with scepticism, assuming it was just another headline stunt. But Maradona pressed the idea with the fierce conviction that had carried him all his life, declaring that the approach was real, that Al Wasl had to believe they could stand among the giants. He dreamed of Drogba leading the line in the heat of Dubai, turning the local league into a global talking point. In the end, he admitted that Drogba's eyes were fixed elsewhere – on the lucrative promise of China – but the point of Diego's ambitions had already been made.

There were also constant clashes with referees. Diego berated officials relentlessly, claiming bias.

Al Wasl finished eighth in the UAE Pro-League – one of the worst performances in the club's history. They also struggled in cup competitions, while controversy, perhaps expectedly, followed Maradona off the pitch, including a suspension for altercations with opposing coaches.

After just a single season in charge, Maradona was unceremoniously sacked by a new Al Wasl board. Following a campaign of unfulfilled promise, the club's previous board had resigned en masse, and the incoming leadership wasted no time: 'Following a meeting … it was decided to terminate the services of coach Diego Maradona and his technical staff,' the club declared. Despite having a year left on his contract and being brought in to raise Al Wasl's profile both on and off the pitch, he was once again without a job.

Maradona did not take the dismissal lightly. He felt betrayed, humiliated. He had believed he could bring joy to Dubai, that his presence alone could elevate the team. In interviews, he lashed out at the directors, claiming they had not given him enough support, that referees had treated Al Wasl unfairly, that politics had played a role.

But privately, Diego seemed weary. He had enjoyed the lifestyle – the sun, the luxury, the adoration. But the distance from Argentina gnawed at him. He missed the madness of his homeland, the raw emotion of South American football. Dubai had been an adventure, but certainly not a home.

Things went from bad to worse for Maradona the following year. In early 2013, he was served with a €39 million tax claim by Italian authorities, rooted in alleged unpaid taxes from his time at Napoli in the mid-to-late 1980s. The notice was delivered while he was staying in Milan, along with a demand that his assets in Italy be frozen to satisfy the debt. Maradona strenuously denied wrongdoing. In interviews he maintained he was being 'persecuted' and insisted he was 'no tax evader'. The saga would ultimately last years. Upon arrival back in Buenos Aires, Maradona was accosted by a sea of reporters at the city's Ezeiza airport, with cameras and microphones shoved in his face as he tried to make his way through. Shouting '*Aguante Boca*!' at the crowd, his patience snapped: he lashed out at journalists, branding them 'blowhards'.

After Dubai, Diego drifted again. Initially he stayed in the UAE as an ambassador for sport, a symbolic role rather than a coaching post. He attended matches and appeared on television. The mayhem continued, but the touchline was silent. Rumours of new jobs never stopped: clubs in Mexico, teams in China, even national sides like Iraq or Iran. Diego entertained them all, but they didn't materialise. The world wanted him present, but not in charge. He was a symbol, not a strategist. Still, he remained Maradona: loved, hated, magnetic. Dubai had not broken him. It had simply added another chapter to the strange odyssey of his post-playing life.

Unable to stay out of the spotlight, he was accused by a celebrity magazine photographer, *Gente*'s Enrique Medina, of kicking him in the groin outside Maradona's father's house. Medina filed a police complaint, claiming

Maradona 'ran at me like he was taking a free kick,' then struck him so hard in the groin and upper thigh area that he 'doubled over in pain'. It made front-page headlines in South America and was repeated in the English-speaking press.

Maradona bizarrely accepted a position with Deportivo Riestra – then a club in Argentina's fourth tier – as a kind of spiritual manager. His role was not the traditional tactical coach. Instead, he delivered motivational speeches, lent prestige and aura to the club, and used his name to inspire players. One report said he flew in, dropped in on training, and handed out a signed shirt with the exhortation: 'Hang on in there Riestra ... win promotion!' Beyond pep talks, he occasionally ran training sessions ('I wanted some fresh air and to have fun watching them play,' he said) and later preseason drop-ins, where he demonstrated free-kick techniques. A widely shared clip captured his hard-edged advice to the squad: '*Si le podés sacar ventaja, sacásela*' ('If you can take an edge, take it').

It was 2014, and the world was watching as Brazil hosted the FIFA World Cup. Expectations hung heavy over Argentina, especially with Maradona – no longer coach, but ever the presence – casting long shadows over every match. He openly criticised FIFA, accusing officials of 'ill will,' and claimed he had been blocked from entering the Maracanã to watch Argentina's victory over Bosnia and Herzegovina. Accustomed to controversy, he insisted he was being punished for speaking truth to power.

His angry outbursts echoed the old defiance of his playing days. He accused FIFA of corruption and claimed the sport's governing body had become a corrupt 'mafia' – something they strongly denied. Despite no formal role, he remained a raging force in public discourse, his voice garage-amplified, his presence impossible to ignore. And although he didn't get into the stadium and was forced to watch the match in the confines of his Rio de Janeiro hotel, Maradona's battles with the establishment struck a sombre chord: not just about whether Argentina would win, but about who controls the game that he and many felt ultimately belongs to the people.

In 2014, as the World Cup unfolded in Brazil, Maradona found yet another stage for reinvention – not on the bench, but in front of the camera. He became co-host of *De Zurda* (*From the Left*), a Venezuelan programme aired on Telesur that blended football analysis with politics, mischief and provocation. It gave him free rein to criticise FIFA, tease its leadership and fire off the kind of sharp remarks that once made press conferences feel like theatre. Watching him, it was clear he had lost none of his edge; *De Zurda* reminded viewers that even without a team to command, his voice still reverberated far beyond the pitch, full of wit, fury and unfiltered charisma.

When Argentina advanced to the final in Rio, Maradona made sure he was close to the action. He checked into the same hotel as the *Albiceleste* in Barra da Tijuca, hovering near the squad as both a symbol and a supporter. To the press, he insisted that Germany were 'beatable' and declared that his country could triumph on South American soil. For the players, it was an unmistakable reminder of the shadow he cast over every generation that wore the shirt.

The night of the final in Rio de Janeiro ended in heartbreak. Mario Götze's goal in extra time sealed a 1–0 victory for Germany, leaving Argentina shattered on the Maracanã turf. Maradona, watching from the sidelines of global television, could not contain his fury. He lambasted FIFA for awarding Lionel Messi the Golden Ball, claiming it was a cynical marketing decision rather than a fair reflection of the tournament. He stressed that while Messi remained a footballing miracle, this accolade felt undeserved – a symbolic gesture designed to satisfy sponsors rather than honour performance.

His anger didn't stop there. He criticised coach Alejandro Sabella for substituting Ezequiel Lavezzi, who had been one of Argentina's liveliest threats down the flank, with Sergio Agüero, arguing that the change disrupted the team's rhythm at the worst possible moment. As ever, his response was raw and emotional: pride for his country intertwined with grief at its defeat. Maradona's lament carried a familiar cadence – wounded patriotism wrapped in theatre – the voice of a man who still saw Argentina's destiny as inseparable from his own. It was pure Diego: fiercely loyal, explosively honest and utterly incapable of retreating into silence when the world's eyes were on the game he loved.

In the aftermath of the 2014 World Cup, Maradona refused to drift into obscurity. He stayed in the headlines through a mixture of football, faith and spectacle. That September, he was one of the star attractions at the Match for Peace in Rome, a charity game organised under the patronage of Pope Francis. Maradona, heavier and slower than in his prime but still capable of moments of magic, set up a goal for Roberto Baggio, rekindling memories of a more glorious past. Away from the pitch, he made a pilgrimage of sorts to meet Pope Francis himself, publicly declaring his admiration for the pontiff and crediting him with restoring his faith after years of detachment. For many Argentines, it was a poignant image: the nation's most notorious son side by side with its most famous spiritual leader.

Yet if his public appearances softened his image, his private life told a different story. In late 2014, Maradona launched a bitter legal battle against his ex-wife Claudia Villafañe, accusing her of mismanaging and misappropriating his fortune. He alleged that she had concealed properties, mishandled memorabilia from his career and cheated him of millions. The case became a media circus in Buenos Aires, drawing tabloid attention and reigniting old tensions between the couple who had once defined Argentina's celebrity culture of the 1980s. For Maradona, who had always lived at the crossroads of football and theatre, the trial was another public stage – one where his grievances spilled into the open, exposing the fractures of his private world.

At a press conference in Bogotá promoting a charity match, Maradona once again made headlines for his words rather than his play. Asked about Louis van Gaal's handling of Radamel Falcao during the Colombian striker's difficult spell at Manchester United, he delivered a typically unfiltered response. He dismissed the Dutch coach in scorching terms, describing him as a man far removed from kindness, closer in spirit to something darker. British newspapers gleefully ran the remark the next morning, another entry in the long catalogue of Diego's verbal explosions. It was pure Maradona – a blend of humour, anger and absolute conviction, spoken by a man who had never been capable of holding his tongue when he felt injustice, especially when it involved one of his own.

Amid the turbulence, he continued to cling to football, though far from the spotlight of World Cups and elite European clubs. He maintained his 'spiritual' advisory role with the modest Buenos Aires side Deportivo Riestra, occasionally turning up at training sessions. It was a strange existence for the man who had once ruled world football: no longer the magician on the pitch, not quite the tactician on the bench, but a restless legend trying to channel his aura into small, unlikely projects. For Maradona, these years underscored how far he had strayed from the life he once imagined – caught between the grandeur of his myth and the stark realities of his present.

More sorrow would find Maradona in 2015. On 25 June, his father, Don Diego, passed away at the age of 87 after suffering heart and respiratory complications. The news shook Maradona deeply. He rushed from Dubai to Buenos Aires, burdened by guilt for not arriving sooner. He later spoke of having been able to say goodbye – to hold his father's hands and touch his face one final time – finding some fragile peace in that moment. He said his father had passed gently, surrounded by his children, enveloped by their love. In a recorded message released days later, Maradona rejected rumours that he had fallen into depression. What he felt, he said, was not despair but the unhealed grief of a son who had lost the man who shaped him. It was an expression of raw humanity from a figure so often seen through myth, a reminder that beneath the legend stood a son mourning in private, carrying the same kind of pain that fame could never soften.

Diego's father, Diego 'Chitoro' Maradona, was a quiet giant in his son's imagination – the steady, unpolished force that anchored a life otherwise defined by chaos and glory. While Diego dazzled the world, Chitoro belonged to another Argentina entirely: the working-class one, the one of sweat, patience and humility. He had spent his days in a chemicals factory, his hands stained by labour, his spirit forged in poverty. Of Guaraní and Galician heritage, he carried within him the mixed history of the country itself – indigenous endurance and European migration, both marked by struggle. Diego often spoke of his father with reverence, remembering a man who had little to give but gave everything nonetheless. He recalled how Chitoro would come home exhausted, clothes still smelling of the factory, yet still find the energy to tell stories, to laugh, to fill the house with warmth. It was from him that Diego learned pride in origins, the stubborn refusal to yield, the belief that dignity could survive even in hardship. Behind every outrageous flourish of the son stood the calm, enduring shadow of the father – a man who never sought the spotlight but became, in Diego's mythology, its quiet foundation.

During the 1980s, when his son reigned over world football, Chitoro became a familiar, fatherly presence around the Argentina camp. He was famous for his *asados*, those long, ritualistic barbecues that in Argentina are less about food than about belonging. While others saw Maradona as untouchable, Chitoro remained simply *el viejo*, the man tending the grill, serving steak and chorizo to players, coaches and staff with the same hands that had once hauled buckets of water and chemical drums to feed his family in Villa Fiorito.

Journalists from the period often noted that when Maradona arrived in camp, so did his father – sometimes with a portable grill in the back of a truck. The players adored him. Jorge Valdano once said that Chitoro's *asados* 'smelled like home', a reminder that the team was still a family, not a brand. Even manager Carlos Bilardo, obsessed with discipline and details, tolerated the informality because he knew how important those gatherings were for team morale. Amid the chaos of fame and the pressure of the game, those *asados* were a sanctuary – the one place where Diego could still just be a son. His father by his side, as always since his teenage years, looked on proudly.

CHAPTER TEN

When the Sand Swallows Applause

THE CAMERA drifted along marble corridors and past mirrored walls, the afternoon sun leaking through gauzy curtains. Somewhere in the distance, a fountain whispered. Then came his voice – unmistakable, slower now, heavier. Diego stood barefoot beside a blue-tiled pool, the Dubai skyline glinting behind him like a mirage. Gone were the crowds, the chaos, the dugouts. What remained was a man addressing the world from his gilded exile, eager to prove he had finally outrun his old ghosts.

In August 2015, Maradona appeared in a video recorded at his home in Dubai, declaring that he had been free from drugs for nearly 12 years. The footage doubled as a tour of his lavish residence – marble floors, memorabilia, and walls lined with photographs of political figures he admired, among them Hugo Chávez and Fidel Castro, the latter of whom he affectionately called 'the greatest man'. At one point, standing by his swimming pool, he turned to the camera with a look of pride and calm resolve. He said he had chosen to live for his daughters, grandchildren and those yet to come, describing sobriety as a daily act of gratitude rather than sacrifice. He reflected that being clean allowed him to wake each morning with clarity, something his years of addiction had stolen. The message felt part confession, part celebration – a man who had survived himself, broadcasting proof of life from a gilded exile in the Gulf.

His self-proclaimed sobriety was celebrated and within 18 months he announced that he had accepted a role with FIFA – a decision that stunned many, given his longstanding hostility toward football's governing body. He took to his Facebook page to declare: 'I can finally fulfil one of the dreams of my life, to work for a clean and transparent FIFA, with people who love football.' His humility there masked the irony: the man who once called FIFA a 'mafia' offered to serve as its emissary. The move was part of a broader reinvention – Maradona, perennial underdog and reluctant insider, once again stepping through the divide between rebel and agent of the system.

Building on his declared aim to join FIFA as a reformer, Maradona surprised many later that same year by re-entering the coaching sphere. In April 2017 he accepted the role of manager at Fujairah FC, a second-division club on the east coast of the United Arab Emirates – his first return to football management since his dismissal from Al Wasl in 2012. Reports said he had joined the club as a technical director, but in truth he was actually the manager.

Fujairah is one of the lesser-known emirates of the UAE, situated on the Gulf of Oman. Unlike the glamour of Dubai or Abu Dhabi, Fujairah is quieter, its economy built on shipping, fishing and oil transport. Its football club, Fujairah FC, had never been a giant of the Emirati game. They had occasional spells in the top flight, but their reality was the second division, fighting for promotion.

The Sheikh who owned the club knew that bringing in Maradona would not suddenly transform them into one of the bigger clubs in the region, such as Al Ain or Al Jazira. But it would certainly bring attention, fill the stands and inspire the players. For a club that normally played in front of very sparse crowds, the arrival of Diego Armando Maradona was like a thunderclap.

Life was more than comfortable in Fujairah. Diego lived in an enormous villa in Dubai, but spent most of his days and occasionally some nights in a luxury hotel near the Fujairah coastline, not far from the team's training ground at the Fujairah Club Stadium. In Fujairah, the pace of life was markedly different: fewer paparazzi, fewer distractions and a modest coastal town surrounded by mountains and desert. He integrated with life in Fujairah more than one would expect. He became a 'keen observer of UAE football', and tried local cuisine frequently. Interestingly, in Fujairah he was introduced to Gaelic football, the national sport of Ireland, when he met with Éire Óg GAA club and posed for photographs.

Diego's methods at Fujairah echoed his style at every other club. Training was less about structure than spirit. He encouraged his players to attack, to play freely, to express themselves. He demanded intensity but often punctuated sessions with humour. He would demonstrate drills himself, still capable of trapping a ball effortlessly, still able to strike passes with precision. The body may have slowed down, but the left foot still had it. But as ever, the tactical framework was loose. Defending was secondary. The shape was fluid. What mattered was energy, bravery and emotion. Diego told them, 'Don't fear mistakes. Fear is the enemy. Attack with love for the ball.'

Fujairah's season in the UAE First Division League began with optimism. Crowds were certainly larger than usual, thanks to Maradona. Local newspapers printed his photo weekly. International media occasionally reported on 'Maradona in the desert'.

He had taken charge and was given one clear objective: win promotion to the UAE's top flight. It looked achievable. In total, he oversaw 11 games, recording seven wins, three draws and a single defeat, a record that suggested progress but fell short of promotion. Despite going on an impressive unbeaten run, a 1–1 draw with Khorfakkan in April 2018 left Fujairah third in the standings – outside the automatic promotion places. Local media ludicrously fumed that those three draws were the hidden cost: too many matches where they couldn't convert dominance into full points.

The club had a chance of promotion via a two-legged play-off. However, within hours of the draw with Khorfakkan, his lawyer Matías Morla announced that Maradona had left the club 'by mutual agreement'.

Behind the polite phrasing, the reality was that the board wanted change. Fujairah later won promotion via the play-offs, but under a caretaker coach. Maradona accepted the decision with unusual restraint, thanking his players and insisting he had been proud of their effort. It was a familiar pattern: a short-lived tenure that carried his aura but ended in frustration, more remembered for the spectacle of his presence than the football itself. Eleven matches, a handful of victories and one more chapter in the restless saga of Diego Maradona the manager.

In the interviews that followed, Maradona remained characteristically defiant. He insisted his time in charge had been a success – that his players had developed, that the team had shown progress and that cruel luck and poor officiating had conspired against them. Yet beneath the bravado there was a flicker of resignation. He admitted that the so-called mutual termination of his contract had, in truth, been more the club's decision than his own. He had wanted to continue, he said, to finish what he had begun, but others had chosen a different path. It was a familiar ending in his managerial life: pride and disappointment intertwined, a sense of unfinished business hanging in the air.

Barely a month later, Maradona was bizarrely unveiled as chairman of Dynamo Brest, a club in the Belarusian Premier League. The appointment made international headlines for its surreal imagery: Maradona waving to fans from a military-style amphibious vehicle during his presentation in Brest's stadium. Officially, his role was as president of the club's board of directors, overseeing 'strategic development', youth projects and marketing. He was expected to act as an ambassador more than a tactician, with the club's vice-chairman explaining that 'his word will carry weight in every decision'. Official statements and multiple press reports indicate that the agreement was for three years and Maradona promised to learn the local language and integrate into life in Minsk by living there part-time.

Belarusian media reported that he was fascinated by the country's discipline and calm, having attended several matches – he told local reporters that 'the people here respect rules, and that is good'.

Still, his time in the role was brief, ending as abruptly as it had begun, which didn't surprise many. By September 2018, after only a few months in post and little tangible impact, he resigned, with a desire to pursue a return to coaching. The grand promises of structure and reform at Dynamo Brest had dissolved into photo ops, headlines and polite goodbyes. He packed his bags once more, restless as ever, the familiar itch returning. He had been a chairman, a politician, a global ambassador – and yet none of it really felt like football. Then came a call from the other side of the world, from a place as far from Minsk as imaginable.

By the second half of 2018, Diego Maradona shouldn't have been capable of genuinely surprising anyone – and yet he somehow kept doing it. The world had grown used to his cycles of chaos and resurrection, of health scares followed by public appearances, of declarations of retirement followed by some new adventure in football's farthest corners. Still, that summer in Russia, during the World Cup, he managed to remind everyone that the theatre of Maradona was a genre unto itself.

Cameras captured him in every emotional register known to man. Before Argentina's do-or-die match against Nigeria in Saint Petersburg, he was seen dancing wildly with Nigerian fans, a grin splitting his face, arms spread in mock triumph, a saint of excess. Minutes later he was crossing himself feverishly, eyes upturned as Messi scored, as if trying to summon divine intervention by sheer will. And then came the collapse – Diego slumped against the glass of his VIP box, his body trembling under the weight of exhaustion, emotion and mythology. Security guards rushed to his aid; soon he was being guided through narrow corridors, helped into a hospitality suite for treatment. The footage went viral, naturally. Within hours, rumours of hospitalisation flooded social media, forcing him to clarify later that it had only been a sharp drop in blood pressure, nothing more. He was alive, again. Always alive.

He had outlived every prophecy of his destruction – the drugs, the cardiac arrests, the scandals, the exiles, the half-rehabilitations that always seemed to crumble back into chaos. Time had tried to claim him, but he kept returning, battered and luminous. So when word broke that *El Diez* – once of Barcelona, Napoli, Boca and the heavens themselves – was coming to coach in Culiacán, even Mexico drew breath.

CHAPTER ELEVEN

The Saint of Sinaloa

CULIACÁN: THE name alone seemed a dare. A city as famous for gunfire as for guava, for blood and baseball and saints with bullet holes in their halos. Capital of Sinaloa, crossroads of the northern desert, home of the most mythologised cartel in the Americas. It sits in a wide fertile valley, where the Humaya and Tamazula rivers meet to form the Culiacán River, running brown and lazy through fields of mango, tomato and suspicion. The heat hangs there like a sentence. By noon the asphalt shimmers, the air smelling faintly of diesel and sweet rot.

To outsiders, the word 'Sinaloa' meant danger: the birthplace of traffickers, the seat of power for Joaquín 'El Chapo' Guzmán's empire. El Chapo was considered one of the most powerful and dangerous men involved in the drug trafficking game in the world at that point. The previous April, the US had imposed its highest, level four 'Do not travel' warning on Sinaloa due to the danger to visitors. For locals, however, it was simply home – a place where *narcocorridos* music played on the radio and everyone knew someone who'd gone missing, but life went on with stoic cheer. They were used to contradictions. So perhaps it was fitting that Maradona, a man made entirely of contradictions, would land there.

Dorados de Sinaloa were the city's football team, born in 2003 from the fever dream of businessmen who wanted to give the region a modern club. Their colours – gold and navy – were meant to suggest wealth and aspiration, though most seasons they looked more like stubborn survivors than princes. They had danced briefly in the Primera División before dropping back to the second tier, Ascenso MX, a place of dust, small stadiums and forgotten ambition. The idea sounded improbable, maybe even reckless – but so did everything Diego ever touched.

The club belonged to Grupo Caliente, the sprawling gambling and casino conglomerate owned by Jorge Hank Rhon. His son Jorgealberto Hank worked for Dorados, and his PR men knew a global brand when they saw one. Hiring Maradona wasn't just a football decision – it was an event, a spectacle, a calculated eruption of fame to draw attention to a team few outside Sinaloa had heard of.

The season had started badly. Dorados were near the bottom of the table, disjointed and dull, and attendance at Estadio Banorte – the tidy 20,000-seat bowl just north of the city – had sagged. A coach's chair sat empty. The phone rang in Buenos Aires.

In late August, Maradona's knees had been throbbing with arthritis while he worked as honorary chairman of Dynamo Brest in Belarus, but his spirit was still wired to the noise of the crowd. The offer from Mexico came wrapped in paradox: money from a gambling empire, a team in the heart of a cartel country. It was madness – and exactly the sort of madness he needed. What's more, Netflix would be documenting every single thing for a series on its streaming service. Diego was still box office.

He confided to a friend in Buenos Aires that he longed to be near the ball again – the one constant in his life, the only thing, he frequently said, that never betrayed him.

He arrived in Culiacán on the evening of 7 September 2018, aboard a small chartered jet. When the door opened, flashbulbs went off like small explosions. The local papers – *Noroeste* and *El Debate* – had run countdowns all week: '*Maradona llega mañana*' ('Maradona arrives tomorrow); '*El Pelusa en Sinaloa*' ('The Fluff in Sinaloa'). Children skipped school to see him. By the time his convoy reached the stadium, hundreds of fans were pressed against the gates, waving Argentina and Boca flags, chanting his name in singsong Spanish.

In the Netflix footage, his arrival carries the weight of a small miracle. The sun blazes over Culiacán, the air thick with heat and anticipation. Diego appears in a Dorados cap and polo, moving stiffly, his body betraying the toll of the years, yet his face lit with that unmistakable energy – half-defiance, half-joy. He moves through the crowd like a man embracing the world, greeting everyone in reach: journalists, ball boys, even the police manning the barricades. When he finally takes the microphone, his voice is rough but commanding. He tells the people of Culiacán that he has not come to parade himself, not to bask in nostalgia, but to work. It is a promise, a challenge and a confession all at once – the pledge of a man who still believes that effort, not myth, can save him.

He gestures to the terraces, where a banner reads '*Bienvenido D10S*' ('Welcome, God', including a play on Maradona's famous number 10). The crowd roars. It doesn't matter that the league is second-tier. For this moment, Culiacán belongs to Diego.

Maradona arrived with a limp, a prayer, and a small entourage that looked more like a rock band than a coaching staff. He didn't bring a full complement of coaches – just Luis Islas, as his assistant. The former Argentina international goalkeeper became his right hand, frontman, foil and sometimes sparring partner.

Islas took charge of training structure and defensive drills. Diego, his knees already failing, couldn't run more than a few steps without wincing, but he compensated with presence. He'd stand at the centre circle, one arm in the air, voice like gravel in wind: '*¡Más rápido, carajo! Vamos, ritmo!*' ('Faster, damn it, rhythm.') Everything was in rhythm. The word became a mantra.

The choice of city still puzzled much of the world. Why Culiacán? Why a team called 'the Fish' (*los Dorados*) in a place where the main sport was baseball and the main export was fear? But to Maradona, the city made metaphorical sense. He had been both saint and sinner, adored and condemned, a man of the poor who lived like royalty and crashed as hard as one can. Culiacán mirrored that duality perfectly: beauty threaded with menace, faith alongside crime.

Some names he recognised had played for the club. Josep Guardiola, the Barcelona legend, finished his playing career there. Former Boca Juniors forward Diego Latorre had a stint in Culiacán. Carlos Casartelli, who Diego had managed in his very first gig with Deportivo Mandiyú back in 1994, also turned out for Dorados at one point.

He drove through town that night in a black SUV, watching the neon flicker across shopfronts: *Farmacia, Caliente Casino, Taquería La Lomita.* Vendors sold T-shirts with his face printed next to the Dorados crest. From a loudspeaker came a *corrido* written overnight by a local band – '*Maradona llegó a Culiacán, con el alma del Diego y el corazón sinaloense…*' ('Maradona arrived in Culiacán, with the soul of Diego and the heart of Sinaloa…')

He looked out the window and muttered to himself, 'It feels like Naples again. But hotter.'

That first week was chaos. Reporters from every continent descended on the city. ESPN, *France24, La Nación, Clarín*, the BBC – they all wanted to see what kind of circus this would be. Netflix's cameras were embedded from day one, following him through training sessions and press conferences. Their tagline – 'Maradona in Mexico: in the heart of the Sinaloa Cartel' – turned a football story into a morality play.

Inside the club offices, executives smiled through the nerves. Dorados's president José Antonio Núñez admitted later, 'We didn't know what to expect. We only knew that everything would change.'

And it did. Within days the training ground in Colinas de la Rivera filled with spectators. Women brought their children to watch him run drills. Vendors set up taco stands at the gates. Players who had spent years in obscurity suddenly found themselves filmed at every warm-up.

The city's mayor welcomed Maradona with an official ceremony, hailing him as a figure of hope and inspiration for Culiacán. Yet beyond the celebrations, not everyone saw his arrival through the same lens. Some national commentators expressed unease, suggesting that the region's deeper issues would not simply disappear in the glow of a global star. Observers noted that Maradona was stepping into a place where football and hardship often lived side by side, a landscape shaped by contradictions. The message was subtle but clear: even someone of Diego's stature was entering a territory that would not be transformed by symbolism alone.

But within the dressing room, scepticism faded. Diego worked as if possessed. Each morning he arrived early, limping across the grass with a cane and a grin, clutching a cup of *mate*. 'Come on, my sons,' he would shout. '*Vamos a meterle ritmo*!' ('Let's put rhythm into it!') He hugged his players, kissed them on the forehead after training.

The local paper ran a headline: *'El amor llegó a Dorados.'* Love has arrived.

Off the pitch, Culiacán responded in kind. Taxi drivers argued about line-ups; schoolteachers hung posters of Diego next to portraits of Benito Juárez. Even the shrine of Jesús Malverde, the so-called 'narco saint', saw a spike in visitors leaving offerings: candles, photos and now, football jerseys. A rumour spread that Maradona himself had visited the shrine in secret, lighting a candle for good luck.

Security around the club tightened. The Sinaloa Cartel rarely touched football – it would be bad for business to do so – but the presence of a global celebrity in their backyard attracted federal attention. Black SUVs with tinted windows began circling the stadium before matches. The players joked that half the crowd carried pistols, the other half cell phones.

Yet the games were joyful. In his debut on 17 September, Dorados thrashed Cafetaleros 4–1, the best performance of their season. The stands shook with chants of '*Olé, olé, olé, Diego, Diego*!' It felt, for a moment, as if the city had been forgiven. At night, Diego stayed in a modest house in a gated community near the stadium. The cameras caught him alone on the patio, sipping *mate*, leg wrapped in ice. 'They told me I'd come to hell,' he says in the Netflix series, smiling at the moon. 'But I see a bit of paradise here.'

The paradise was fragile. Culiacán's underworld didn't pause for football. In November, gunfire erupted downtown after a cartel boss was captured. The next morning's headlines shared space: '*Violencia en Sinaloa*' above a smaller line – '*Dorados gana otra vez*' ('Dorados wins again'). Life went on, both stories true.

Still, Diego gave people something else to talk about. Vendors sold '*D10S de Sinaloa*' shirts. Graffiti appeared near Parque Las Riberas: '*La pelota no se mancha.*' ('The ball doesn't get dirty.') That phrase – his old line from 2001 when he retired at Boca – became his new credo in Mexico. He repeated it at press conferences whenever journalists asked about the cartels, adding, '*El fútbol es lo más limpio que temenos.*' ('Football is the cleanest thing we have.')

The truth was more complicated. His boss's empire thrived on gambling revenue; his pay-cheque came from the same machine that fed Mexico's vice industry. But Maradona seemed immune to irony. For him, sincerity was a form of resistance. Culiacán's people read him the way they read their own city: flawed, brilliant, impossible to ignore. When he wept after victories – arms lifted, eyes to the sky – they saw not performance but recognition. He understood their hunger. 'He speaks like us,' said one fan outside the stadium. 'He fights like us.'

By the end of September, Dorados had climbed the table. The town's evening noise changed: fewer gunshots, more fireworks. The cafés along Álvaro Obregón played highlights on repeat. Even the police at checkpoints at the city's entrances began wearing Dorados scarves. For once, football was giving baseball a run for its money in Culiacán.

When asked why he had chosen to come, Diego offered a simple answer. 'Because no one else would,' he said. 'Because they believed in me.' And that, perhaps, was the heart of it. Culiacán believed because it had been judged and dismissed a thousand times. Diego believed because he had been judged and dismissed a thousand more. The meeting of those two outcasts – one a city, one a man – was never about salvation. It was about recognition.

On the night of his first home win, he walked slowly around the pitch, arm-in-arm with a young ball boy. The crowd stayed long after the final whistle, chanting his name until the lights went out. From the mountains beyond the city, the sound echoed like thunder. For the people of Culiacán, Diego Maradona had come not to cleanse them but to mirror them – flawed, radiant, defiant. And for a fleeting moment in that feverish September, it worked.

As October unfolded, the Maradona effect in Culiacán deepened. The explosion of energy from September's debut had to be turned into consistency. The club and the media pushed narratives of a 'rescue mission' made real. A press profile in ESPN later noted that in the first six games before he arrived, Dorados had scored just two goals; under Maradona in subsequent matches they began to average far more. Players, staff and observers refer to October as the month when belief consolidated: the idea that this team could compete, not just survive.

At Dorados's modest training base in Colinas de la Rivera, the pitches were patchy, ringed with palm trees and power lines. The facilities had none of the gloss of Europe or Buenos Aires – a few small dressing rooms, a gym the size of a convenience store. But Diego made it feel like Boca Juniors. He demanded music, laughter and noise. He banned headphones at breakfast. 'We talk to each other here,' he said. 'Not to machines.'

In *Maradona in Mexico*, there's a telling scene early on: he strides into the changing room before training, claps his hands and shouts, 'Good morning, my champions!' The players – many still shy around him – echo back a nervous 'Good morning, coach.' He laughs. 'No, no, like lions! Again!' It's both theatre and theology. His leadership is tactile, emotional, musical.

Islas, ever the pragmatist, ran the training sessions with stopwatch precision, yet even he conceded that Maradona carried something intangible. When Diego walked into a room, he said later, a charge of energy seemed to sweep through it – faces lit up, voices lifted and suddenly everyone felt alive again.

The roster he inherited was a typical Ascenso blend: veterans chasing one last contract, kids on loan from Tijuana or América, a handful of journeymen who had bounced across Latin America's lower leagues. The team's heart comprised a trio of players: Gaspar Servio, an Argentine goalkeeper with tattoos up his neck and a fierce grin; Vinicio Angulo, a wiry Ecuadorian striker who ran like he had fire in his lungs; and Jorge Córdoba, a lanky forward whose finishing was as unpredictable as a slot machine.

Servio vividly recalled their first meeting. Maradona embraced him as if greeting an old friend and told him with complete conviction that he was his goalkeeper, that he trusted him completely. It was a moment unlike any other in Servio's career – no manager had ever offered such faith before a single training session.

Trust became Diego's currency. He didn't speak to his players about tactics so much as about life: about betrayal, poverty, hunger, pride. Before matches he'd pace the locker room, quoting Perón one minute and street slang the next. 'Don't do it for Maradona,' he told them before one away game, captured in the Netflix series. 'Do it for football. For your mothers. For the kids watching.'

It wasn't polished rhetoric – his sentences sometimes broke into mutters – but it worked. The players began to run harder, fight longer. They said later that they didn't want to disappoint him.

The early weeks were a honeymoon. Dorados, once aimless, suddenly played with swagger. The ball moved more quickly. The press pushed higher. Islas organised them into a compact 4-4-2, but Diego encouraged improvisation in attack. '*Si ves el espacio, ocupalo.*' ('If you see the space, take it.') '*El fútbol no es ajedrez, es tango.*' ('Football isn't chess; it's tango.')

During one training session, the young American Rubio Rubin missed a sitter and kicked the turf in frustration, starting to walk off. Diego limped over, put an arm around his shoulder and whispered, 'Always end on a good note. Never finish on a bad shot.' He handed him another ball. 'Again.' Rubin scored. Maradona smiled like a proud uncle and said, 'Now you can go.'

It was that human connection – part psychologist, part street philosopher – that turned a struggling club into a cause. Within a month, Dorados climbed from the bottom of the table into the play-off race. Culiacán's stadium, once half-empty, now sold out every weekend. Fans travelled in convoys from Mazatlán and Los Mochis to catch a glimpse of the legend in gold.

But the euphoria wasn't just on the field. It was social, almost religious. In a city where headlines usually belonged to gunfights, Maradona's antics became redemption stories that occasionally bordered on the ludicrous. Local radio carried breathless segments: '*Diego viste de dorado... Diego baila con su equipo ... Diego abraza a los niños enfermos.*' ('Diego dresses in gold ... Diego dances with the team ... Diego hugs sick children').

Everywhere he went, he crossed boundaries. When he attended a Tomateros de Culiacán baseball game, the stadium erupted in applause; when he met the governor, reporters counted the seconds before Diego cracked a joke about corruption. 'In Argentina,' he said, 'they steal too, but they smile less.'

At training sessions, he wore caps emblazoned with *Viva México*, and by December he'd picked up enough local slang to sound half-Sinaloense. He called his players *plebes* – lads. He drank coffee sweetened with condensed milk, the way the locals did. It was as if he was absorbing the city's rhythm into his bloodstream.

Still, the body was betraying him. His knees had ballooned. Between sessions he needed cortisone injections just to walk. In the Netflix footage, there are quiet moments that undercut the bravado: Diego alone in his room, groaning as he pulls on his trousers, whispering a small prayer. 'I have pain every day,' he says. 'But when I'm on the pitch, it disappears.'

Luis Islas often acted as both assistant and guardian. He'd help him up stairs, keep press away when Diego was exhausted. But their relationship frayed over time – too much passion, too little rest. They'd argue over substitutions, over hotel schedules, over whether to rest certain players. 'We were two lions in one cage,' Islas said later.

Media giant ESPN ran a light-hearted feature about his 'new life in Mexico', describing him trying local risotto and joking with chefs. The man who once ruled Naples was now embraced as an adopted *culichi*, the local demonym for residents of Culiacán. Yet, as always with Maradona, the line between charisma and chaos was thin. After a narrow defeat in October, he gave a post-match interview that went viral: 40 seconds of silence, blinking, searching for words, before delivering a meandering critique of the referee. *Sports Illustrated* called it 'bizarre', but to his players it was vintage Diego – a man who felt everything too deeply to form neat sentences.

The league in Mexico, like in Argentina, was played in an *Apertura* and *Clausura* format – two separate half-season competitions, with the *Apertura* (opening) played in the early months of the season, followed by the *Clausura* (closing) contested in the latter half. Dorados entered the *Apertura* play-offs as underdogs.

Against Mineros de Zacatecas they played one of their finest games: Angulo scored twice, Servio saved a penalty and Diego wept on the bench, hands trembling. The cameras zoomed in on his face – not just joy, but something like relief. He had found meaning again.

Behind the scenes, Culiacán's peculiar machinery adapted around him. Security doubled; federal police coordinated travel routes. The Hank family's PR team churned out glossy press releases about 'hope and transformation through football'. At night, the casinos of Grupo Caliente filled with customers watching Dorados replays on overhead screens. The house always wins.

Diego either didn't know or didn't care about the contradictions. He lived by the ball. In one press conference, when asked about cartel violence, he answered, 'The only war I fight is on the field. The ball unites; bullets divide.' The phrase ran on front pages across Latin America.

That December, after Dorados lost the final in heartbreaking fashion – conceding to Atlético San Luis in extra time – he erupted at fans who taunted him from the stands. Security footage shows him lunging forward, shouting, before being restrained by staff. It was pure Diego: incandescent love, followed by incandescent rage. The disciplinary committee fined him, but in Culiacán, it only deepened the myth.

The following week, instead of sulking, he hosted a Christmas party for the squad. There was a barbecue, *cumbia* music, beer and an endless line of hugs. He gave each player a signed Dorados shirt with the words '*Gracias por creer*'. ('Thank you for believing'.) That was his genius: to turn failure into fraternity. 'We didn't win the title,' said Servio later, 'but we became a family. He made us feel invincible.'

By January, the new *Clausura* season began under heavy expectation. Luis Islas abruptly resigned – his reasons never fully clear, 'End of an excellent cycle. We achieve results and goals with work and a very clear soccer idea! I wish you the best Diego! Dorados fans will accompany you a lot here too', the former goalkeeper shared via Twitter. Maradona, publicly, thanked him and carried on. He promoted José María Martínez from within the staff, a quieter figure, and told the press: 'The music doesn't stop. The dance goes on.'

Without Islas' structure, the sessions grew looser, more intimate. Netflix's *Maradona in Mexico* captures it beautifully: Diego sitting on an ice chest in the centre of the pitch, talking to players about life, not tactics. 'Don't waste a single training session,' he tells them. 'You don't know when football will say goodbye.' Big words. Deep words. Maradona, like every footballer, knew that the transition into retirement isn't easy. Take nothing for granted.

The second campaign mirrored the first: slow start, furious surge. Behind the scenes, Diego's health deteriorated. The cameras caught him wincing as he climbed the dugout steps, staff slipping ice packs under his tracksuit at half-time. The *LA Times* described him that spring as 'a man moving on determination more than bone'. Yet his players insisted he was tireless. Goalkeeper Gaspar Servio told *Clarín*, 'He'd arrive at seven in the morning, in pain, but smiling. If the boss can suffer like that, how can we not give everything?'

In public, Maradona was the same kaleidoscope of moods – kissing fans one day, berating referees the next. During one post-match in February, after a 3–2 win, he looked straight into the cameras and shouted, '*¡Esto es para la gente de Culiacán, que sufre y trabaja todos los días!*' ('This is for the people of Culiacán, who suffer and work every day.') The phrase ran on banners the following week.

Dorados finished the *Clausura* regular season fifth, enough to qualify for the *Liguillas* (play-offs) once more. The club's transformation was beyond dispute: two consecutive *Liguillas*, two bursts of national attention, and a city that now treated home matches as civic festivals. Vendors outside the stadium sold shirts reading '*Fe en Diego*' ('Faith in Diego').

The quarter-final brought déjà vu: another two-leg dogfight with Cafetaleros de Tapachula. Dorados advanced 6–3 on aggregate, Angulo scoring twice. In the semis they edged out Mineros de Zacatecas again, this time on away goals. The atmosphere around Estadio Banorte turned quasi-religious. Before each match, Maradona led the players in prayer: heads bowed, arms interlinked, his gravelly voice reciting the *Padre Nuestro*. 'For me,' he said later, 'God is on the pitch.'

The final was destiny's cruel reprise. Once again, Atlético San Luis awaited. The first leg, on 2 May 2019, was played in Culiacán under suffocating heat. Dorados took a controversial lead when the referee awarded a penalty for hand ball – though replays showed the ball had struck a defender's face. *AS México* called it '*el penal más polémico del año*' ('the most controversial penalty of the year'). Jorge Córdoba converted. Moments later, San Luis equalised through Juan Castro. The 1–1 draw left everything open.

The second leg, on 5 May 2019, was suffused with fatalism. At Estadio Alfonso Lastras, 25,000 fans packed the stands. From his technical area, Maradona gestured wildly, his knee bandaged, shouting tactical fragments: '*¡Cierre! ¡Presione! ¡Toquen rápido!*' For 90 minutes Dorados resisted and the score remained 0–0, so extra time followed. In the 103rd minute came heartbreak: goalkeeper Servio failed to collect a corner, the ball dropping for Unai Bilbao to stab home. San Luis won 1–0, securing back-to-back titles and promotion to Liga MX.

As the home crowd celebrated, Maradona slumped on to the bench, head in hands. Netflix's cameras lingered on his face – anguish, disbelief, then a kind of weary smile. '*Lo dimos todo*,' he murmured. ('We gave everything.') In the press room he refused to blame anyone. 'The boys left their souls out there,' he said. 'Football sometimes gives, sometimes takes away.'

Fate seemed to mock him. Yet in the city, he had already won something subtler. Culiacán, long defined by shadows, now had an idol in sunlight. Children wore Dorados jerseys instead of those of European clubs. Local artists painted murals: Diego surrounded by golden fish, Malverde watching from above. 'Maradona came to the land of the bullet,' one columnist wrote, 'and gave us back the ball.'

Defeat did not feel like failure. The local paper *Noroeste* wrote, 'Dorados fell with honour. Maradona has restored the name of this club.' Fans gathered outside the stadium with candles, singing, '*Gracias Diego*.' For a city used to headlines of bloodshed, mourning a lost football final felt almost redemptive.

In the weeks that followed, Maradona's condition worsened. He underwent tests with a view to having shoulder and knee surgery, doctors warning that without operations he might soon be unable to walk. Still, he posted videos from his home thanking fans. 'I love Culiacán,' he said. 'You treated me like one of your own.'

On 14 June 2019, Dorados released a brief statement: 'Due to medical orders, Diego Armando Maradona will not continue as manager of Dorados de Sinaloa for the upcoming season. The club wishes him the best recovery.'

He left quietly, no press conference, no farewell match. According to *FMF State of Mind*, 'after two finals in two seasons, he departs a hero'. Sky Sports summarised it simply: 'Maradona leaves Mexico after leading Dorados to successive finals.'

Culiacán reacted as if he'd died. Murals bloomed overnight – Diego in gold, hand over heart, haloed by rays of yellow paint. One inscription read, '*Gracias por el milagro que no fue*' ('Thank you for the miracle that never was').

In interviews later that year, several Dorados players admitted they were still coming to terms with his absence. Rubin told ESPN that Maradona's lessons went far beyond tactics – he taught them about attitude, resilience and the small rituals that built confidence, such as insisting they always finish training on a high note. Servio remembered the embraces after every match, the gentle kisses on the forehead, the way Diego made each player feel valued. Even in defeat, he said, Maradona had a gift for making them believe they were champions.

For Maradona, the Mexican chapter became one of the last coherent acts of his life. It gave him purpose again, a daily rhythm of hope and exhaustion. When he spoke about it later, already back in Argentina, he called those months '*una resurrección pequeña*' ('a small resurrection').

From a purely footballing angle, the record is extraordinary: *Apertura* 2018 runners-up. *Clausura* 2019 runners-up again. Two finals, 36 matches, 18 wins, and a goal average nearly double what Dorados had managed before him. But the real transformation was cultural. Dorados became a mirror for their coach – imperfect, volatile, magnificent. They had learned, in his words, to 'play with heart, not fear'.

The Netflix series immortalised it: the broken genius, still giving everything, still fighting, still living for football. *Maradona in Mexico* was not about tactics or trophies. It was about humanity. A flawed man, in a flawed city, finding redemption together – even if only for a year.

When he left Mexico, Maradona promised he'd return one day to thank the fans. But the legend remained: the saint and the sinner who turned a forgotten club in the heart of cartel country into a symbol of redemption. For those who were there, the memory endures in noise and colour – the roar of Estadio Banorte, the smell of fireworks and the sight of a limping, grinning man in gold raising his fist to the sky as if to say, 'We nearly touched heaven.'

CHAPTER TWELVE

The Last Pilgrimage

ASIF KAPADIA'S 2019 documentary *Diego Maradona* – the third in the British director's informal trilogy after *Senna* and *Amy* – assembled more than 500 hours of unseen archival footage to tell the story of Maradona's tumultuous rise and fall in Naples. The filmmaker obtained the material from two Argentine cameramen who had been commissioned in the 1980s to film Maradona's private life for a never-completed project. The result, shaped from home videos, match reels and news footage, is a portrait of duality: 'Diego', the fragile, funny boy from Villa Fiorito, and 'Maradona', the indestructible idol invented to survive Naples, drugs and global fame. The film traces his arrival at Napoli in 1984, the *scudetti* (his Serie A league titles), his entanglement with the famous mafia outfit, the Camorra, his 1991 drug ban and the slow drift into chaos. Kapadia refused voice-over narration, letting the images and contemporaneous audio tell the story; the effect is both intimate and forensic.

Maradona initially played along, giving interviews from Dubai while Kapadia's team painstakingly digitised the lost footage. He spoke warmly about the film's ambition, saying he hoped it would reveal the real man behind the myth. During one session, Kapadia found himself seated beside Maradona's legendary left foot and, unable to resist, reached out to touch it – an impulsive gesture that visibly irritated Diego. When the film finally premiered at Cannes, his response was mixed. He later complained that it lingered too much on his chaos and too little on his redemption and family, telling *Clarín* it showed his life with too much sorrow and not enough joy. Kapadia maintained that the turmoil and genius were inseparable, two sides of the same story. Critics, meanwhile, hailed the documentary for its candour and construction, calling it operatic and perhaps the most complete portrait yet of a footballer who lived as if forever shadowed by his own legend.

After the release of *Diego Maradona* in 2019, and following his emotional departure from Dorados, Maradona's hunger to remain near the game refused to fade. Even as his body faltered, he saw coaching as both medicine and mission – a way to stay alive within football's rhythm. From his home in Buenos Aires, he began fielding offers from Argentine clubs, eager for a return to familiar soil after years in exile. '*Además, quería pasar mis últimos años en Argentina*,' ('I want to spend my last years in Argentina') he said in one televised interview. The chance arrived that September, when Gimnasia y Esgrima La Plata, languishing at the bottom of the Superliga, asked him to take over. To friends, it felt inevitable: after wandering through the deserts of Dubai and the dust of Culiacán, Diego

Armando Maradona was coming home to rescue one last lost cause.

By now, he moved significantly more slowly, battered by decades of excess, limping from surgeries, bloated by medication, his voice rasping, his eyes tired. Yet in that fragility he became something even greater than a player or a coach: he became an object of adulation, of collective catharsis, of national veneration. Every stadium he visited turned into a temple. Every rival became a mourner-in-waiting. His final year on the bench was Argentina's chance to embrace him while he still lived, to transform football matches into public confessions of love, to tell Diego one last time that he was theirs. And he, even in weakness, gave them that gift.

Gimnasia was not a glamorous destination. It was a club defined by struggle. Founded in 1887, older even than giants like River Plate and Boca Juniors, it was historically a team of the people, a badge worn by labourers and students in La Plata, but not one weighted with silver. Estudiantes, their bitter rivals across town, had hoisted Libertadores cups and Intercontinental trophies. Gimnasia had none of that. They were proud, noisy, faithful, but always the underdog, always the strugglers. In 2019, they were fighting relegation, a squad short on quality, a fan base weary of despair. They needed hope more than results. They needed someone who could bring them belief.

When word spread that Maradona would become their manager, the city erupted in disbelief. Could it be real? Diego Maradona, world champion, god of

Naples, coach of Argentina, descending into the mud of relegation with humble Gimnasia? It sounded like fantasy, yet it was true. The club confirmed the hiring on 5 September, while noting that Gimnasia was plunging toward relegation in the Superliga. He replaced Darío Ortiz, who had left three days prior, and an interim duo (Leandro Martini and Mariano Messera) held the reins for that brief period before Maradona's arrival. At his presentation the next day, in front of thousands of fans at the Juan Carmelo Zerillo stadium, Maradona was visibly emotional. He pledged to fight to save Gimnasia's season.

He admitted candidly that he could offer no guarantees, reminding everyone he was no magician – that if emotion alone could win matches, the crowd's welcome that day would have been enough. The reception was overwhelming; within days, the club had sold out its new shirts and seen a dramatic surge in membership, proof that his arrival had already transformed Gimnasia's fortunes off the pitch before a single ball was kicked.

The first weeks were unforgiving. His debut came on 15 September 2019, a 2–1 defeat to Racing Club, followed by further losses to Talleres and River Plate. The press called it a cruel start, but even amid defeat, crowds kept swelling. Then came flickers of resurrection: a 4–2 win at Godoy Cruz, a 4–0 triumph over Newell's Old Boys and a 3–0 victory over Aldosivi – results that briefly lifted Gimnasia from the bottom and seemed to justify the madness of hiring Maradona. Still, inconsistency ruled. The team lacked the tactical balance and squad depth to sustain a run, and Diego's touchline charisma couldn't mask systemic flaws. They played for him, but didn't yet know how to win.

Off the field, his first three months were a mirror of Argentina's chaos: passion colliding with politics. Gimnasia's survival was still uncertain, but its soul had been reawakened. The club was losing less, believing more, and Maradona, in his old tracksuit, hands trembling and eyes bright, had once again turned despair into devotion. However, his future became entangled in internal club elections – he vowed to stay only if president Gabriel Pellegrino was re-elected.

By mid-November, Maradona's tumultuous spell at Gimnasia had reached its inevitable breaking point. The club was still hovering near the foot of the table despite flashes of revival and his position had become inseparable from the outcome of the upcoming presidential elections. True to his word, when it appeared that Pellegrino would not stand for re-election, Maradona announced his resignation. The news detonated across La Plata: fans poured into the streets, waving banners that read '*Diego no se va*' ('Diego isn't leaving'). Thousands surrounded El Bosque in protest, demanding his return, and within 48 hours Pellegrino brokered a fragile truce between rival factions. In an Instagram video, the 59-year-old confirmed he would stay, thanking supporters 'for making me feel loved once again'. The political storm had temporarily calmed, and the legend was back on the touchline, his job saved not by results or directors, but by the devotion of the people who refused to let him go.

The results remained erratic. Gimnasia still dropped points, still conceded soft goals and still teetered near the relegation line. Yet somehow, the scoreboard had ceased to be the story. What mattered now was the feeling – the shared theatre of it all. Each match unfolded like a national ritual rather than a football game. Journalists called it 'the Maradona effect': an ordinary club turned into a travelling stage for Argentina's deepest devotion. Cameras clung to him; every shrug, grimace and grin became front-page material. It wasn't management anymore – it was a ceremony.

The pilgrimage spread far beyond La Plata. When he took his Gimnasia side to Rosario, to play Newell's Old Boys – the club he had briefly graced as a player – they placed a throne painted red and black beside the pitch and invited him to sit upon it like a returning king. Maradona smiled through damp eyes as tens of thousands chanted his name. Across the country, from Independiente to Vélez, from San Lorenzo to Córdoba's fierce Belgrano, rivals laid down their grudges and offered applause, flowers and banners. For once, Argentina's most divisive figure became its binding one. Everyone sensed the twilight approaching, and for a fleeting season, even his enemies wanted to say thank you.

By March 2020, the tension that had surrounded Maradona's turbulent months at Gimnasia y Esgrima La Plata reached its crescendo – and fate conspired to bring him home. The final day of the Superliga placed him back at La Bombonera, the stadium of his youth, his glory, his legend. Boca Juniors – the club of his life – were fighting for the title, needing a win and a favour from fate to overtake River Plate, their eternal and bitter rivals, who were playing simultaneously in Tucumán. The night carried the weight of history and farewell; every camera, every eye in the ground seemed fixed on Maradona's return to the place where his myth had first burned brightest. Then, before the match began, came the moment that turned drama into folklore: Carlos Tevez, Boca's captain and Maradona's spiritual heir at Boca, crossed the pitch to the visiting bench and planted a quick kiss on his idol's lips. Deep into the second half, Tevez would score the goal that sealed the championship. The kiss became legend – a gesture that fused past and present, turning rivals into kin and the night into a national fable. 'I kissed Diego because he gives you luck,' he told the media, treating the gesture as part superstition, part homage.

There was deep history behind that moment. Tevez – the 'Apache', born in Fuerte Apache – and Maradona – the 'Diez', raised in Villa Fiorito – shared more than a footballing language. They came from the same world: poverty, street pitches and the stubborn will to rise above circumstance. In the stands, Juan Román Riquelme, the gifted *enganche* who is still an icon with Boca, and with whom Maradona didn't see eye-to-eye, now a club director, watched the scene with a half-smile, half-grimace – another symbolic image in Boca's mythology. The Bombonera itself seemed to pulse with mixed emotions: reverence for Maradona, anxiety about the title. Gimnasia arrived fighting relegation, but under Diego they played with dignity, determined not to be extras in another team's celebration. The story practically wrote itself: Maradona, Tevez, Riquelme: three of the club's most famous number 10s all together on one night where Boca won the title, even if the most famous of them all, Diego, was with the opposing team.

Although results had very slightly improved since his arrival in September 2019, Gimnasia were still saddled with the threat of falling into the second tier when the Argentine season was prematurely cancelled in April due to the global Covid-19 outbreak; fortune intervened when the national association voted to suspend relegation that year, allowing Maradona's side to remain in the top flight. The club's message to him – 'For us, you are one more *Tripero* (Gimnasia supporter) and your heart is as blue and white as ours' – was as much political as footballing, a declaration that the La Plata-based club's identity now intertwined with his own.

Despite a season plagued by inconsistency, relegation fears and external turbulence, Maradona remained at the helm of Gimnasia. In June 2020, the club announced an extension of his contract, to keep him through the 2020/21 campaign – despite persistent doubts about the team's capacity to survive.

Diego Maradona's 60th birthday on 30 October 2020 fell in the midst of the global pandemic, which complicated the usual public celebrations. Yet Argentina still turned the day into a kind of national fête. A giant 100m billboard with his face was installed along a central avenue in Buenos Aires, near the Obelisk, as a public tribute to his life and legend. He also used the day for reflection and projection. In interviews around that date, Maradona spoke of a whimsical birthday wish: that he might score another goal against England – this time with his right hand (a playful reference to his famous 'Hand of God' goal in 1986). In those media appearances, he emphasised that his greatest pride was the joy he had given people through football. FIFA's own site paid tribute by highlighting the many moments in his career.

Two days after the milestone occasion, Maradona was admitted to a private clinic in La Plata amid reports of depression, poor appetite and general malaise – signs that his spirits and health were failing. Medical sources noted he had been 'very sad for a week' and had stopped eating, prompting his personal physician, neurosurgeon Leopoldo Luque, to arrange hospital diagnostics. In the days following admission, everything shifted: an emergency brain operation was required after imaging revealed a subdural haematoma, a dangerous collection of blood between the skull and brain membranes.

The surgery, performed at the Olivos clinic just outside Buenos Aires, was declared a success: Luque reported that he'd evacuated the haematoma completely and that Maradona had tolerated the procedure well. Doctors confirmed there was no immediate neurological damage and no post-operative complications. Maradona was monitored closely, kept hospitalised for days to manage the fluid drain and slowly but gradually moved into recovery mode, though part of his medical team acknowledged he was also dealing with withdrawal symptoms tied to long-standing alcohol dependency.

His recovery from the brain surgery took a brighter turn within days, when Luque told journalists that Maradona had 'laughed, looked at me, grabbed my hand' – small gestures, but huge signals in a post-operative setting. Though cautious, the medical team moved in tandem. They removed the drain, coordinated closely with intensive care specialists and emphasised that Maradona's recovery would need to be evaluated day by day.

Maradona was discharged from the clinic on 11 November. He was moved to a rented house in a gated residential area in Tigre, around a 40-minute drive north from the centre of Buenos Aires, for home convalescence. There, he was reportedly under the care of a medical team including his neurosurgeon, a psychiatrist, psychologists and nursing staff.

Argentina watched anxiously. News channels gave daily updates on his progress, quoting family members, speculating about his moods. He was described as restless, depressed and frustrated. His closest circle insisted he was fine, that he was eating, walking, smiling. But leaked details suggested otherwise: that he occasionally resisted medication, that he wanted to be left alone, that he sank into melancholy. The pandemic made visits difficult. His isolation grew. And all the while, the nation held its breath.

CHAPTER THIRTEEN

The Echo That Never Ends

MORNING IN Buenos Aires. The city's early heat was already pooling, shimmering across pavements and gathering in the leafy avenues. Jacaranda blossoms, vivid purple, drifted through the air, falling like confetti on parked cars, on cracked sidewalks, on the airy façades of old houses. Inside a rented home in the gated *barrio* of San Andrés, in Dique Luján, part of Tigre, Diego Armando Maradona lay in convalescence – the stage set for a final act long anticipated but never accepted.

His brain surgery had been deemed, by his doctors, a success. Yet success is a fragile thing in a body already weathered by years of excess, illness, emotional storms and a lifetime of contradictions. The home had been set up for recovery, with a network of caregivers and medications. But the canopy over that care was fragile, cracked.

By late morning on 25 November 2020, the narrative arc that had shadowed Maradona's later life – illness, treatment, relapse, charisma, fight, decline, relapse again – gathered momentum toward its final escalation. Around midday, according to the sequence later assembled by investigators, his psychiatrist and psychologist arrived for a scheduled visit and found him unresponsive. The moment was quiet but decisive, like a fuse burning down in secret.

An emergency call was quickly placed, time-stamped soon after noon. Within minutes, paramedics and ambulances converged on the gated house. They tried to revive him – CPR, defibrillations, every measure they could bring – but to no avail. At approximately 13:10 local time, one doctor on site pronounced him dead. The early forensic assessment – one that would soon emerge in preliminary reports – delivered a diagnosis that, in its clinical language, echoed the whispers of the last years: acute pulmonary oedema, his lungs overwhelmed by fluid; a battered, dilated, enlarged heart so weakened it could no longer cope; underlying dilated cardiomyopathy and chronic heart failure. The toxicology revealed a cabinet's worth of prescription psychotropic drugs (the product of long medical struggles), but no illicit narcotics. In that modest room, in that borrowed home, the life of Argentina's greatest footballer went silent.

The news quickly became public, thundering across media circuits and for a moment, the country stopped. '*Diego Armando Maradona ha muerto de un paro cardiaco.*' ('Diego Armando Maradona died of cardiac arrest.') *Clarín*, who had tracked every detail of Maradona's health since his brain surgery earlier that November, was first to break it: *Murió Diego Armando*

Maradona. The paper would later boast of having the *primicia mundial* – the global scoop – while other outlets quickly followed. At 13:16, Radio AM750 interrupted its regular programming to confirm the death. People across Argentina turned to one another, disbelieving. Something impossible was suddenly real. Radio stations broke into obituary bulletins. Television anchors, unaccustomed to being seen so raw, choked back tears live on air. And then the silence shattered: into wailing, into chants, into grief so overwhelming it spilled into the streets.

Within an hour, the story had ceased to be mere information; it had become atmosphere. The news hung in the air like weather – inescapable, total and already rewriting the world that had existed an hour before.

The State responded with ritual, immediate and commanding. Within hours, the presidency declared a national mourning period of three days. Plans were quickly laid for a wake in the Casa Rosada, the presidential palace overlooking Plaza de Mayo – the same plaza that had witnessed so many Argentine ecstasies and traumas, and the same plaza where Maradona, triumphant in 1986, had cradled the World Cup trophy, lifting a nation. On television, the anchor's cadence slowed as though pulling gravity into speech itself. Across the city, people gathered: homemade banners, images of Maradona, crowds swelling where news cameras pointed. The image that spread most virally was electric: two Argentine fans, one in a Boca Juniors shirt and one in a River

Plate shirt – bitter rivals on the pitch – embracing each other, tears flowing. Only Diego could gather foes into one grief.

The morning after – the Thursday – Buenos Aires awoke to a city rearranged, as if shaken free of its usual shape by grief. The streets felt uneasy, hushed in the early light, as though the city itself were holding its breath. People emerged onto the neighbourhood corners, the plazas, into the old cafés, wandering in a post-Maradona world. The reality had begun to settle, heavy, sticky.

Before sunrise, the Casa Rosada opened its doors. The pale light filtered into its halls where the coffin lay: draped in Argentina's sky-blue and white flag, flanked by the shirts that had in many ways become identity garments – a jersey from Argentinos Juniors, another from Boca Juniors, and the sacred *albiceleste* number 10 of the national team. Under chandeliers glowing with heat that the morning had already summoned, the body rested in state. The line that formed to pay respects began in darkness and did not relent.

By dawn, thousands had already joined – men and women of every generation, some carrying tears in their eyes, others phones raised to capture a moment they knew would be historic. Children too young to remember 1986 walked alongside parents who spoke of Diego as if he had once been their neighbour, their confidant. Poor men in weathered clothes murmured his name as a sermon. The queue snaked through Plaza de Mayo, spilled into adjacent streets, stretched into the city's guts. Buses came early. People arrived from provinces, from distant towns. The air pulsed with something between mourning and worship.

Inside, in the Salón de los Patriotas Latinoamericanos – that venerable hall within Casa Rosada reserved for state rituals – his coffin lay in a regal yet intimate posture. This gallery of Latin American patriots, where the statues of San Martín and Belgrano stand in solemn silence, had been transformed into a chapel of farewell. The symbolism was electric: a man both myth and mortal passing through the same halls where Argentina punctuates its memory of heroes.

Outside, the city roared. Chants broke like waves: '*Diego no murió, Diego vive en el pueblo.*' ('Diego didn't die, Diego lives in the people.') The message was unambiguous: Maradona might have left flesh, but his spirit was eternal, immortal in collective devotion. Fans pressed forward, seeking glimpses of the coffin, of his face hidden beneath cloth and light. The sun climbed; the heat rose. Yet the line, always crawling, resisted.

By midday, tension was rising. The patience of thousands began to fray as the crowd pressed forward, the energy building like steam in a sealed vessel. Police lines strained; barriers gave way. In the courtyards, fans tried to force entry into interior patios and in some corners the passageways to the inner galleries were completely overrun. Inside the Casa Rosada, Maradona's family, watching the chaos unfold, grew fearful. They made the painful decision to end the public wake early. What had been intended as a full day of national mourning became a sudden, hasty departure.

The cortege then left the Casa Rosada, slow and deliberate, transforming the farewell into a procession across Buenos Aires. Along Avenida 9 de Julio and the surrounding streets, Argentines gathered shoulder to shoulder, waving flags, lifting scarves and singing through tears. As the coffin passed, the air filled with grief and reverence. The atmosphere was suspended somewhere between euphoria and sorrow, a collective performance of devotion. Many who watched felt that something elemental had shifted, as if the country itself was losing a part of its heartbeat. People emerged on to balconies and pavements, hands over hearts; cars stopped; cyclists pulled aside. The noise fell away into a hushed, trembling silence.

Eventually, the convoy wound its way out of the city toward Jardín Bella Vista Cemetery, on the outskirts of Buenos Aires, where his parents – Dalma Salvadora and 'Don Diego' – were already buried. It had long been assumed that Maradona would rest beside them. The ceremony that followed was quiet, almost hidden from view. Only close family and friends were permitted to attend. The graveside was small, the light fading as dusk fell. The burial was understated, intimate, a muted farewell rather than a spectacle.

It was not the ending Argentina had imagined – no grand stadium tribute, no mass procession carrying him aloft like a trophy. Instead, the farewell was shaped by necessity, by the sheer weight of the multitudes pressing too close. Yet there was a strange poetry in that. For decades, Maradona had pulled the nation toward him with magnetic force; in death, his family was forced to push it gently back. For 40 years they had tried to touch him. On this day, his loved ones drew a final, fragile line of separation.

In that divide between private ritual and public mourning lay the emblem of his life: a man who belonged to everyone, whose death demanded both closeness and protection. The intensity of the crowds threatened to turn grief into spectacle and the family, aware of that danger, curtailed what might have become an uncontrollable scene. Still, they could not contain the emotion entirely. Inside the Casa Rosada, in the streets and in homes across Argentina, the mourning had already begun its unstoppable course.

After the burial, the city seemed to exhale – raggedly, unevenly. In bars, cafés and living rooms, people traded stories: of the goals, the wild celebrations, the moments that felt like miracles. Songs returned to the air; old chants resurfaced. On television, the footage rolled without pause – Diego as a child in Villa Fiorito, Diego in Naples, Diego crying as the anthem played in Mexico. Around the world, tributes poured in: stadium lights dimmed, players wore black armbands and jerseys bearing his name appeared in shop windows and on screens. In Naples, torches lit up the night. In Argentina, flags dropped to half-mast.

But because his death had become a national drama, questions quickly followed. Could it have been prevented? Was the home care sufficient? Should he have been under hospital supervision? Within days, prosecutors opened an investigation into potential negligence, charges were brought against seven health professionals. Their first court case was declared a mistrial in May 2025 and at the time of writing, a new trial was expected to take place in March 2026. The debate grew to encompass medicine, ethics and the unbearable expectations placed on those who cared for a man treated as immortal.

Through it all, the deeper truth remained: Argentina felt as if it had lost a part of its soul. A coffin was lowered beside his parents under the evening sky while a nation stood outside, singing, crying, refusing to let go. The chaos and reverence distilled the paradox of his existence – Diego Armando Maradona had always been more than flesh, and even in absence, he filled the air.

In those days, Buenos Aires resembled its own sacred stadium. The Casa Rosada seemed to transform into La Bombonera – flag-draped, sunlit, tumultuous. Tributes were everywhere. *Página/12* described it as an *adiós multitudinario*, a farewell made of thousands moving as one. The AFA declared seven days of mourning for Argentine football and every match began with an extra minute of silence that somehow contained all the noise of his life. Across continents – in Tegucigalpa, in Naples, in small-town pitches across Europe – black armbands, photographs and applause echoed the same grief. It was tempting to reach for metaphors – Diego the saint, Diego the sinner, Diego the comet – but what happened in those days was simpler and truer: the ordinary labour of love, expressed in queues, songs and tears.

The scenes were immense and intimate at once: women clutching posters as if relics, fathers showing their children the murals painted overnight. At Boca's stadium, banners stretched across terraces bearing his words, *La pelota no se mancha* (the ball doesn't get stained) now transformed into an epitaph. Within days, the club had painted his face across the stands he once commanded. The television coverage became a continuous vigil, a day and night of replayed memories: goals, laughter, rebellion and grace. Diego reappeared everywhere – on screens, in murals, in the voices rising from the streets. Death had not diminished him; it had multiplied him.

The contradictions of his life also spilled into the debates about his legacy. Some voices, quieter but insistent, reminded people of his flaws: his substance abuse, his chaotic family life, the controversies with women, the political outbursts. But even these voices were drowned in the wave of adoration. Argentina had chosen, in those days, to forgive, to embrace the whole man with all his shadows. The funeral chants said it clearly: '*Diego no murió, Diego vive.*' ('Diego didn't die. Diego lives.') They did not mean that literally. They meant that in memory, in identity, in the collective soul, he would never die.

Across the ocean, Naples had begun a vigil. Newspapers in Italy rearranged their front pages; *La Gazzetta* ran photographs from 1986 and from Spaccanapoli, the road in the city where he still peers down from murals. Mayor de Magistris turned grief into an administrative motion: rename Napoli's home stadium after Maradona. A week later, the city council made it official: the stadium where he bent the physics of a football match would carry his name. In a city and a country where Catholicism is so strong, it is incredibly staggering that they renamed the stadium after Maradona, given that it was previously named after the apostle, St Paul. The Vatican said Pope Francis 'recalls with affection' their meetings and 'remembers him in prayer', an unusually personal papal note for a footballer.

Also in Naples, graffiti artists took to the crumbling Murale di San Giovanni a Teduccio and repainted it, restoring, brushstroke by brushstroke, Maradona's youthful grin. The mural, once weathered and eroded, reclaimed a vigour in mourning's service.

Lionel Messi distilled the country's mood into one line: 'Diego is eternal.' At the Camp Nou, during Barcelona's 4–0 home win over Osasuna in La Liga, in the 73rd minute Messi scored from outside the box – left foot, top corner – and then pulled off his Barça shirt to reveal the red-and-black number 10 jersey of Newell's Old Boys, the Rosario club where he is from, that Maradona had briefly played for in 1993. He raised both arms and looked skyward before crossing himself. The referee booked him for removing his shirt, but the image circled the planet: the quietest and most eloquent salute of that week. After the match Messi wrote on Instagram: '*Hasta siempre, Diego.*' ('Farewell forever, Diego.') Pelé, the only other footballer who lives in the same mythic weather system, said: 'I have lost a dear friend. One day, I hope we will play football together in the sky.'

In Seville, where Maradona had spent a season with Sevilla, flags were lowered in solemn tribute. The Andalusian city remembered a time when the small, fierce Argentine dribbled across its pitches, leaving footprints in local memory. In London – a city which had never quite forgiven the 'Hand of God' goal of 1986 – the outpouring was unexpected, even cathartic: newspapers that had once portrayed him as provocateur now printed superlatives, calling him 'the greatest' and celebrating the genius that so many could not ignore.

Among those to speak was Gary Lineker, who had shared the field with Maradona in 1986 and later appeared alongside him in a BBC documentary. Holding back emotion, he said that watching Diego play felt like watching someone touch the divine. In his tribute he recalled a moment in a dressing room: Maradona, in nothing but shorts, was juggling his socks on one foot for minutes before walking on to the pitch and astonishing everyone. 'I've never seen anyone have such a beautiful affection with a football,' he said.

Across continents in Asia, Africa, the Americas, tributes poured in. In Berlin, a mural appeared overnight; in New York, the side of a building was painted with his silhouette; in Dublin, a mural appeared close to the Irish national team's stadium; in Tokyo and Barcelona, walls bloomed with images of his face; in Cape Town, murals declared him immortal. In Rio de Janeiro's Vila Cruzeiro *favela* – home to fierce football devotion – a large mural depicted Maradona in his Napoli years, arms outstretched, a testament that rivalry could yield respect. Even in Brazil, where football is religion and Argentina an eternal rival, Maradona's aura crossed boundaries. Sporting bodies and federations offered condolences; matches paused for a minute's silence, clubs displayed his number 10 on screens and jerseys.

Even in Kerala, India, where Maradona had toured and had touched football's fringes, fans mobilised swiftly: within days, plans were announced to erect a grand statue, and proposals for a 'Maradona museum' emerged. A Kerala jeweller announced a life-size gold sculpture planned to evoke the 'Hand of God' goal as its focal piece. In Kolkata itself, a 12ft bronze figure was unveiled (though it drew controversy for its lack of likeness).

In a world of rival clubs and fierce allegiances, the loss was universal. The world had lost not just a player, but a voice – a tempest in cleats, a man who challenged the limits of possibility. The murals, tears and tributes became more than homage: they were the chorus to a final, resonant verse in the legend that was Diego Armando Maradona.

The conversations in Argentina circled endlessly around what his passing meant. Some said he was the last unifying figure of the country, someone who had carried everyone regardless of politics, class, or club. Others argued that he represented Argentina's contradictions: brilliance and chaos, triumph and scandal, humility and arrogance. Intellectuals filled pages with essays about his symbolism. Journalists wrote of him as a mirror of the nation. Yet in homes and on the streets, the message was simpler: he was ours, he gave us joy and now he is gone.

Football itself seemed diminished. Matches were played in silence for him, with minutes of applause or silence before kick-off, players standing with bowed heads, coaches with tears in their eyes. At Boca Juniors, La Bombonera became a shrine. Supporters placed flowers at the gates, filled the streets around the stadium with chants and turned the famous murals of Diego into altars with candles and shirts. At Gimnasia, the stadium where he had coached his last games, supporters sang all night, as if the sound could reach him in the afterlife. Even River Plate's Monumental, once the hostile ground where Diego had been booed as a Boca idol, now displayed messages of respect. For a rare moment, Argentina's football family was whole.

Argentina, naturally, felt it most deeply because Diego had always been their mirror. His rise from the shacks of Villa Fiorito to the summit of the world game had embodied their hope. His battles with addiction, with scandal, with politics, had embodied their flaws. His genius and his sins belonged to them equally. And now his death reopened all the contradictions: pride and shame, love and anger, grief and gratitude. The psychologists on television said Argentina was experiencing a collective trauma, a grief on the scale of Evita Perón's funeral in 1952. Politicians declared him a national hero. Writers spoke of him as myth, as saint, as demon. Ordinary Argentines said simply: 'We have lost our Diego.'

The debates about his legacy grew louder as the immediate shock passed. Was he the greatest footballer of all time? Was Messi his equal, or his superior? Did his off-field chaos diminish his achievements, or did it make them more human, more real? The arguments filled newspapers and airwaves, but beneath them was the recognition that statistics and comparisons could not capture him. He was not just a footballer but an event, a phenomenon, a life that exceeded the sport. To speak of his goals was to speak of joy itself. To speak of his scandals was to speak of pain and contradiction. He embodied everything, the whole spectrum of human existence. That was why his death felt so profound.

On the evening of Sunday, 29 November 2020, just four days after Diego Maradona's death, La Bombonera – the sacred ground that he loved most – despite being closed due to the global pandemic, became a cathedral of mourning. Boca Juniors hosted Newell's Old Boys, and the match itself turned into a living requiem. In the *palco de Diego*, the private box he had occupied for years, sat his eldest daughter, Dalma Maradona, dressed in a Boca shirt and wearing a face mask. At full time, the players ran toward the touchline, laid a Maradona number 10 shirt on the turf, and applauded toward her father's box. She broke down in sadness and gratitude.

Through December, tributes multiplied. The funeral's emotional aftershocks did not fade – they reverberated. FIFA released a commemorative video montage, narrated by Gianni Infantino: 'What Diego gave to football cannot be measured. It is infinite.' The phrase took on a liturgical cadence, as fans played it again and again, letting it settle like a benediction over mourning stadiums.

Near the Obelisco – Buenos Aires' great monolith and symbolic heart – a fan camp persisted through Christmas. The centrepiece was a shrine: an altar of candles, banners, scarves, flowers and a handwritten sign that read, '*Te lo juro, Diego, no te vamos a olvidar nunca*' ('I swear to you, Diego, we will never forget you'). The shrine was semi-informal, living. Authorities would occasionally clear the site under public order pretexts, but the moment they walked away, fans would return, new candles, fresh notes, fresh tears. The shrine's persistence became part ritual, part defiance. It turned into a pilgrimage locus for both locals and visitors – people came with small tokens: jerseys, handwritten letters, even childhood toys they placed near the candles. Social media amplified the images: night after night, lamps glowed, flags fluttered and in the video loops one would see faces pressed near the shrine, illuminated by flickering flames.

Elsewhere, across Argentina and beyond, the tributes took manifold forms. In Bella Vista cemetery, graffiti inscriptions like '*Aquí descansa D10S*' ('Here rests D10S'), became rallying texts of devotion. In many towns, local football clubs renamed tournaments, painted murals on stadium walls and held remembrance matches. The Argentine Football Association (AFA) announced that the 2020 Copa de la Liga would be renamed the Copa Diego Armando Maradona, immortalising him in the institutional calendar.

In the weeks that followed, essays, books, exhibitions and television specials proliferated. In cafés and bars, fans gathered to debate whether Maradona's flaws magnified or softened his myth. The multimedia memorialisation turned him into a perpetual presence: in TV retrospectives, archival interviews, goal compilations, mythic retellings. The boundary between memory and spectacle blurred.

By January, the world was littered with Maradona's echoes. The candle shrines, the murals, the stadium dedications, the renamed cups – these were not just acts of mourning; they were acts of possession, of claiming a piece of him for the living. In that way, Diego Armando Maradona transcended death: not as a ghost, but as a force that continued shaping streets, stories, identities.

The intellectuals of Argentina and abroad filled columns with reflections on his legacy. Writers compared him to Evita, to Che, to Ali, to other icons who transcended their fields. Some argued he was the purest symbol of the South: a boy from poverty who challenged the rich, who fought against the North, who gave dignity to those who had none. Others argued he represented Argentina itself – brilliant, self-destructive, resilient, proud. There were essays about his politics, his friendship with Fidel Castro and Hugo Chávez, his anti-imperial speeches, his tattoos of Che and Fidel. Some criticised him for aligning with dictators, others celebrated him for defying the powerful. Yet all agreed that he could never be reduced to a simple figure. He was too vast, too contradictory, too alive even in death.

The younger generation, those who had not seen him play live, found him through Messi, and through Messi the legend was renewed. The debates between Messi and Maradona raged louder after his death. Was Messi the better player, the more complete, the more disciplined? Or was Maradona greater, because he embodied struggle and carried teams beyond reason? In truth, the debate mattered less than the continuity it created. When Messi lifted the Copa América in 2021 at the Maracanã, ending Argentina's 28-year drought, the cameras caught him weeping and fans shouted Diego's name as though he had been present on the pitch. It felt like a victory shared across time, as if Maradona had whispered into Messi's ear from beyond, blessing him to complete the story. When Messi later lifted the World Cup in 2022, the images of him holding the trophy were immediately placed side by side with Diego's in 1986. The circle had closed: Argentina's two greatest sons, united by destiny, carrying the same cup in different centuries. And in that, Diego's eternity was secured, because every mention of Messi carried the shadow of Maradona and every comparison to Messi resurrected him.

Yet for all the debates, the essential truth was simple. Diego lived on in every child who kicked a ball on a street in Buenos Aires, in every chant of '*¡Olé, olé, olé, olé, Diego, Diego*!' that erupted spontaneously in a stadium, in every mural, every candle, every whispered story. He was not just a ghost of the past but a presence in the present. Teachers told schoolchildren about him not as a distant figure but as part of their lives. Families told stories of where they were in 1986, passing down memories like inheritance. The country itself seemed to rearrange its mythology around him. San Martín was the liberator, Perón was the populist, Evita was the saint and Diego was the eternal.

His managerial career, which this book has followed in detail, was remembered less for tactics than for emotions. From Mandiyú to Racing, from Al Wasl to Fujairah, from Dorados to Gimnasia, the results were often poor. But his presence elevated the ordinary into spectacle. In Dubai, he turned a minor club into world headlines. In Sinaloa, he gave hope to a region scarred by violence. In La Plata, he transformed Gimnasia into the centre of a national farewell. His managerial career was not about winning. It was about reminding people of his existence, about sharing himself with those far from the glamour of Europe. He gave his presence to the humble, to the forgotten, to the places where joy was scarce.

The people who had known him personally told stories that only deepened the myth. Former teammates recalled his generosity, the way he would give money to strangers, buy meals for the poor and invite children from slums into training camps. Friends told of his humour, his endless pranks, his capacity for laughter even in pain. Nurses and drivers spoke of his tenderness, of the way he thanked them, of the way he listened to their stories. These small testimonies joined the larger narrative: that Diego, for all his chaos, carried a huge heart.

In Argentina, debates erupted about how to teach future generations about him. Schools organised exhibitions. Museums planned permanent displays. Documentaries multiplied. The Netflix series about his time in Mexico, the Asif Kapadia film, the countless books and articles – all became part of an expanding canon of Maradona studies. He was no longer just a footballer but a subject of history, culture and theology. Scholars analysed his religious cult, the Church of Maradona, which celebrated him with its own rituals. Priests debated whether he should be considered a form of folk saint. In *barrios* across the country, people lit candles before images of him and prayed not only for his soul but for their own lives, asking for his intercession in moments of struggle. He had become more than mortal.

And yet, despite the grandeur, his essence remained simple: a boy with a ball. The clips of him juggling oranges as a child, playing barefoot on muddy fields, dancing with the ball tied to his foot, circulated endlessly. That was who Diego was at heart – the boy who loved the game, who found freedom in the ball, who said that football was the only thing that made him feel close to heaven. His eternity was built not only on trophies and scandals but on the pure joy of play. That was what people clung to, what they remembered most vividly: the smile on his face when he touched the ball. And the brilliance.

Eternity is not measured in trophies or statistics. It is measured in memory, in presence, in the ability to linger in the soul of a people long after the body is gone. Diego Armando Maradona had not been perfect: he had been fragile, reckless, excessive, self-destructive. But in those very flaws he had mirrored Argentina itself, and that was why, in death, he became eternal. His goals against England, his triumph in Mexico, his victories with Napoli were etched in film and replayed endlessly, but what remained deepest was the way he made people feel: the goosebumps in the Azteca, the shouts of joy in the streets of Naples, the tears in La Bombonera when he returned for the last time. He had given people joy, and joy is the greatest gift.

In the end, what remains are the images: the boy juggling a ball on dirt fields in Villa Fiorito; the teenager dazzling at Argentinos Juniors; the young man in Boca blue running to the terraces; the genius of 1986 dancing past England; the captain lifting the World Cup in Mexico City; the god of Naples standing on balconies, arms raised; the weeping man in 1994 after being expelled from the World Cup; the defiant coach screaming at journalists in 2009; the father-figure embracing players in Mexico and Argentina; the frail old man sitting on a throne in Newell's, smiling through tears; the fragile coach embraced by Carlos Tevez at La Bombonera; the coffin draped in Argentina's flag carried through the streets of Buenos Aires as the people cried his name. A life of images, a life of contradictions, a life of love.

And so the story closes not with silence but with sound – the sound of chants echoing from the far corners of Argentina to every hamlet whispering his name. The eternal chorus arises: '*¡Olé, olé, olé, olé, Diego, Diego!*' – a refrain that will never entirely fade, because even in absence the crowd continues singing. Maradona is dead, yes – but he is everywhere.

He lingers now in the spin of a ball at a child's foot, in that clumsy first touch which time and repetition will refine into grace. He lives in the shared memory of a nation – in alleyways, courtyards and plazas where his name once burst from open windows in celebration. His image watches over Naples from its walls, fading and flaking, yet somehow more alive than paint should allow. For the poor and the dreamers, he endures as a prayer of rebellion – proof that destiny can be defied. He resides, too, in the archives: in grainy film, in the pages of record books, in the eternal myth of the game itself. He is timeless because he belongs not only to history, but to every moment that follows it.

As long as football exists – as long as children imagine, as long as the number 10 carries a trace of magic – his shadow remains. In the darkness of a packed stadium, in the hush before a ball is struck, in the single heartbeat of collective breath, he is there. He once said that when he stepped on to the pitch, life vanished, everything else dissolved. In that realm of floodlights and pressure, stripped of every disguise, he found happiness – and he gave it back to millions.

He was more than a footballer; he was a distortion in time, a spark that briefly bent the natural order of the sport. His genius was not only in skill but in how he redefined what could be done – slipping past defenders, gliding through space, turning chaos into geometry. The 'Goal of the Century' against England in 1986 remains immortal not just for what happened, but for how it felt: as though, for ten seconds, a mortal had outrun the laws of physics. And beside that miracle stands its twin – the 'Hand of God' – an act of cunning and faith that captured all his contradictions: sin and sanctity, deceit and brilliance, all in one gesture.

Maradona was never spotless, and that imperfection was part of his radiance. He fought addiction, illness and the crushing weight of adoration. He stumbled often, repented, fell again, and somehow kept rising – propelled by the same fire that once ignited stadiums. His greatness was born from volatility; his beauty, from pain. The divine and the broken coexisted in him and that tension made him indelible.

This is not an ending, but an echo. The chant of his name still drifts through *barrios* and piazzas, along cracked concrete and perfect grass, through the tunnels of old arenas where his spirit hums against the stone. Fathers tell their children about the nights they saw him play – for Boca, for Napoli, for Argentina – their eyes shining in the retelling. The footage will roll on for generations and he will keep astonishing them, because true brilliance never ages; it only changes form.

From the narrow streets of La Boca to the makeshift fields of Naples, children will chase the ball and shout his name into the dusk. And in those fleeting instants – when joy outruns reason – he will live again.

'I'm a player who has given joy to the people,' he once said. 'And that's enough for me.'

Diego Armando Maradona

30 October 1960 – 25 November 2020

Afterword from the Author

I WAS seven years old in the summer of 1990, when the World Cup finals in Italy were about to take place. It was Ireland's first time at the finals and the spirit had transformed the country into one of ecstasy and joy. I grew up in a neighbourhood in south Dublin which had a local park with a boxing club and a concrete five-a-side pitch. Every young boy had a football at his feet during the tournament. I was no different.

I was playing football with my dad in our back garden when suddenly – BANG – a wallop of the plastic ball smashed me in the face courtesy of his right foot. I had never felt such pain and fear. I vividly recall falling over and crying. I probably thought, '*This is the worst thing to ever happen. I'm probably going to die from these injuries.*' My dad, worried his wife would hear the commotion, needed this crying seven-year-old to stop.

'Ah, will you get up,' he said before realising he should add something more inspirational to get me off the ground. 'Maradona took a bang of a football to the face and he just got on with it. He's a great player.'

I remember precisely that warm afternoon when he said it, though I can't recall why the moment felt so significant at the time. The air was still, heavy with the scent of cut grass and summer dust, and my father's voice carried across the small back garden like a challenge. I barely knew the names of the Irish players then – just Packie Bonner, the heroic goalkeeper, and Paul McGrath, whose name carried a quiet kind of strength. But I had heard the name Maradona somewhere, spoken with the kind of reverence usually reserved for myth. The World Cup was approaching, Ireland's first ever, and every newspaper, television and radio broadcast seemed to hum with anticipation. Amid all that noise, one name kept surfacing – Maradona. I didn't yet understand that he was more than just a footballer, that he was the most famous player alive, a man who seemed to belong as much to legend as to the game itself. When my dad invoked his name, urging me to rise from the mucky grass, something shifted – a spark of curiosity, a sense that beyond our narrow patch of earth lay a wider, electric world where names like that carried power. *Who was this man exactly?*

I watched that World Cup in relatives' living rooms, the kind of crowded gatherings where the adults worked their way through cans of lager and cider while the kids – usually me and one or two of my older sisters – sat glued to the screen in a fog of cigarette smoke. Ireland rode the wave all the way to the quarter-finals, only to fall narrowly to Italy thanks to Salvatore 'Toto' Schillaci. Had we somehow upset the hosts, the next opponent waiting in the semi-final would have been Maradona's Argentina.

From that summer onward, something in me shifted. I began to watch the Argentinian player with a fascination that bordered on obsession. He wasn't just another name on the television anymore; he was a figure I followed with the curiosity of someone discovering a myth unravelling in real time. I remember his goal against Greece in the 1994 World Cup as vividly as if it happened yesterday – the ball rocketing into the top corner, his face twisting in a kind of electric ecstasy, those wild, bulging eyes staring straight into the camera, almost manic. It wasn't just a celebration; it was a declaration, the kind of moment that burned itself into memory. And then, only days later, came the fall. I remember the English papers gloating with a cruel delight when FIFA banned him.

When he rejoined Boca Juniors in 1995, I had almost no way of seeing him play. The world still felt enormous then, and Argentina might as well have been another planet. All I had was a 20-second clip on a Channel 4 morning sports programme – a grainy montage of global highlights that, for a fleeting moment, showed him back in the blue and gold, the crowd at La Bombonera shaking like thunder. That glimpse was enough to plant something permanent.

In the years that followed, I hunted for him wherever I could find him. Old VHS tapes of mid-1980s Serie A games passed between friends, bootleg DVDs bought at car boot sales, late-night highlight reels and, eventually, the boundless frontier of internet streaming – all of it brought Diego a little closer, frame by frame. Only then did I begin to see the full scope of what he could do: the sudden burst of acceleration, the impossible balance, the way he could make a football seem tethered to his will. It was art disguised as chaos.

The more I watched, the more I understood that his genius wasn't neat or predictable – it was raw, mercurial and deeply human. Every touch seemed to carry a story. Diego was, and remains, my favourite player.

Those familiar with my work or who follow me on social media know of my admiration for Boca Juniors – the club he is synonymous with, and vice versa. I used to lie awake late at night with a laptop, getting goosebumps when the camera turned to Maradona in his box, passionately screaming at the players below, and the crowd erupted in chants of his name.

I've been to La Bombonera three times (only once for a match), and I consider myself lucky to say that. The stadium is renowned all over the world, mostly because of Diego. The same goes for La Boca, the working-class neighbourhood where it stands. I've purchased numerous Boca jerseys over the years, most of which include the famous number 10. When I presented my last book to the Cultural Department of Boca Juniors at La Bombonera in early August 2025, they in return presented me with a Boca jersey with my name on the back of it alongside the iconic number 10. I didn't feel worthy to have my name alongside such a sacred footballing shirt number in that stadium.

When Maradona died in 2020, I was devastated. The incredible Asif Kapadia documentary *Diego*

Maradona had been released just a year earlier, thrusting him back even more into public consciousness in the English-speaking world. I took to Instagram and wrote: 'RIP D10S. Diego Armando Maradona 1960–2020. The greatest.'

I meant it. I still do. Maradona was the greatest. I know, I know – some of you reading this will argue he's not even the greatest Argentinian. Some will bring up Pelé, Ronaldo, Beckenbauer, Cruyff, Zidane, Charlton, Best, Di Stéfano and others. But to me, Maradona had something extra.

I have a couple of Maradona tattoos on my arms. I wouldn't suffer that pain and expense for many, but for him I would – and indeed I have. (Also for the Dude from *The Big Lebowski*, and for the bands The Cramps and The Beatles.)

He was a flawed individual in many ways, but those in his presence knew they were with greatness. It should have rubbed off on the players he coached, but it never did. The gulf between Maradona the player and Maradona the coach was cosmic. His managerial career, by any measure, amounted to a faint echo of what he had achieved with a ball at his feet – not even five per cent of his playing greatness, as some analysts cruelly but accurately observed. Yet even in failure, he remained impossible to dismiss.

He had been a simple boy from the *barrio*, a bona-fide genius, and even in his latter years, he was undeniably still a god.

About the Author

Rob Smith is a musician, DJ, producer and occasional writer. He holds a long-standing residency at the renowned Dublin music venue, The Workman's Club. He has played or DJed in various places around the world, from Berlin to Buenos Aires and from Newcastle to New York.

He occasionally records music under the name The Swedish Railway Orchestra, currently signed to the label Blowtorch Records.

He is a devout fanatic of Boca Juniors.

He currently lives in Ireland with his wife and daughter.